Lifting the Chaderi

My Life as an Afghan Refugee

By Anisa Mahmoud Ulrich

Lifting the Chaderi: My Life as an Afghan Refugee
Copyright © 2012 by Anisa Mahmoud Ulrich
ISBN-13: 978-1-4699-4572-9
ISBN-10: 1-4699-4572-X

Published by Two Worlds Press, San Ramon, CA
Cover design: Lisa Drittenbas, author photo: Ashley Nichole Ulrich
Cover background photo: John Scott Rafoss

This book is a work of nonfiction. The stories are true, but some names and places have been changed to protect the privacy of family members and friends.

This book is available on Amazon.com.

~ *Dedication* ~

This book is dedicated to my mother and father. They were, indeed, the most courageous people in my life. I thank them for having confidence in me, even though the bravery they instilled meant I had to leave them.

This book is also dedicated to my aunt Sofia, who was like a mother to me during tough times. She was my faithful traveling companion over the Torkham pass into Pakistan.

To my brother Zaman, who had the patience and courage to guide us on those harsh roads: the journey could not have occurred without your leadership and strength. We have had our difficult moments, but nothing can weaken our love and compassion towards each other and our faith in family.

To my oldest brother, Amir, the rough and tough one, who has a kind heart and loving spirit: I know we will never forget where we came from and how much we suffered as children. I know you just want me to be happy and are always watching over me.

To my whole family, I want you to know how much I love you from the bottom of my heart, no matter what differences we may have encountered over the years.

Finally, I want to thank my wonderful mother for giving me that big heart of hers. I am truly blessed, and will never forget her tenacity in life and her love of family.

~ ~ ~

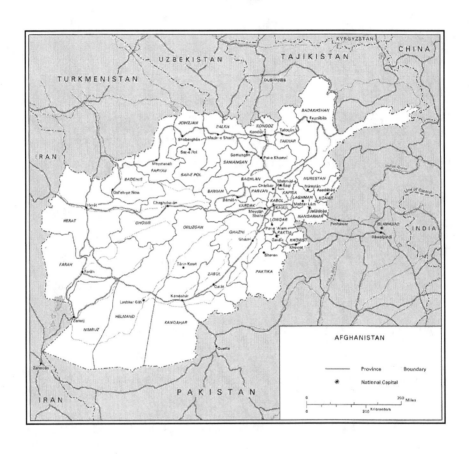

AFGHANISTAN

Province ———— Boundary

● National Capital

~ Introduction ~

In April of 2010, I was on a plane to Afghanistan. This was my third trip to Kabul since 2005. Before then, I had not been home in twenty-five years. The last two flights were mostly full of Americans and aid workers. But this time, there were Afghans on board. I talked to some of them, and they all had journeys similar to mine: they were refugees, returning to see their families. Some after two years, some after twenty years.

We were not that high above the ground, and I could see the Sharki Baratayi Mountain down below, looking rugged. The sky was blue with a few clouds here and there. We were getting closer to home, and it felt exhilarating. Everyone was looking out of the little windows with smiles on their faces. I knew exactly how they felt.

It's the feeling of familiarity, of belonging to our sweet land, where we once lived in peace and harmony. In those days, we all lived close to our families and friends. We had jobs, homes, mothers and fathers, brothers and sisters. We had weddings, parties, graduations and picnics.

When I was growing up in Kabul in the 1960s, my aunts, uncles and grandparents were always visiting. We would gather around my grandfather after dinner, sit on cushions on the floor while we drank tea and ate candy, walnuts and raisins, and he would tell us fairy tales night after night. He normally stayed two or three nights at our house, and each day, I looked forward to another night with my grandfather and his stories. It saddened me every time he left our house. Then, we didn't have TV or any other means of entertainment, so we craved those story nights.

A couple of my aunts were also the storytellers of the family. I loved it when they came to visit, too. I used to go to my aunts' farms, with my mother, who we called *Bu bu-jaan*, or *Mami*, and my oldest sister Pari. We loved seeing the cows, sheep, goats, and chickens, and hearing the roosters singing in the morning. My aunts would bake their white flat bread, fresh every day, and cook lamb with rice and fried eggplant or spinach or corn on the cob. We would take these delicious dishes and picnic along the Shewakee River, sitting under the berry bushes and cherry trees. I remember climbing those trees like a tomboy and picking cherries.

It is thirty-one years later, but I still remember those moments, and I can't stop crying for my mother, father, family, and my beautiful Afghanistan. Even though my family struggled at times, and didn't always get along with each other, that is where I was born and raised, and that is the world I am from.

More than thirty years of war have destroyed our land: first Russia, then the Mujahidin, and finally, the worst of all, the Taliban. They made Afghanistan the war zone of the world. They created the hiding places (caves) for them and their weapons, and grew and sold poppies for the drug addicts of the world, the sale of which would provide for guns and bombs, and more supplies for war.

This was the nightmare of the courageous people of Afghanistan. They went through hell and lost so much. Families were broken up. Refugees, like my family and me, fled to different parts of the world. Now we have our freedom, jobs, homes and new lives, but no matter what part of the world we find ourselves in, we all have one thing in common: we dearly miss our home and our land.

~~~

We were getting closer to Kabul. The mountains were covered with white powdered snow, sparkling in the sun. I didn't see too many houses though, as it was mostly mountains and desert, and did not have much greenery at all.

After we landed at Kabul airport, the women were assisted through security first, since women are shown respect in that way. As we were waiting for our luggage (which took two hours), a young man ran to help me with my carry-on and wait for my bags. He brought me a cup of coffee and let me use his phone to call my brother Aman, who was waiting for me outside the airport with my sister and nieces.

"Salaam, my dear sister. How was your flight? We are waiting for you outside the airport since we are not allowed inside. We will see you when you come out."

"Salaam salaam," I said to Aman. "My flight was good." As usual, I had a lump in my throat from the excitement of being back home.

While I was waiting, I had a vision of organizing a clinic or school here in Kabul. I definitely know what to name it. It would be called, "Bee bee Mariam," after my mother, because she was my hero. "Bee bee" is a prefix often used, especially for religious women. I want her name to last forever, because it was her persistence and hard work that got us where we are now.

She didn't even have a formal education. The only book she

could read was the Quran in Arabic, and she didn't even know what it meant. Beyond anyone I have ever known, though, she had such a craving for education for all of her children.

My mother put up with so much grief from our conservative relatives, who didn't believe in educating girls. Of course, they didn't complain about my brothers going to school – they were permitted to do so. That didn't stop her from letting us continuing our education. *Mami* said, "the hell with them," and tried not to let it bother her.

She took my sister Zaybah and me to the Zahishga Nurse Midwifery School, wearing her *chaderi* (the long cloak that covers women head to toe, with only a small mesh of fabric to see out of), and enrolled us. She wanted us to become nurse-midwives to help people, and to become independent, because she wasn't. We were the first females in both my parents' families to finish college. My mother struggled to make ends meet, but she made sure we had food and all the necessities, and she was always there for us.

I have now been a labor and delivery nurse for over twenty-five years, and I have attended hundreds of births. Sharing the beautiful moment of a child being born into the lives of new parents, and devoting my life to taking care of people, gives me a sense of fulfillment. I can proudly say that the sacrifices my mother made to ensure our education were successful.

~ One ~

Mother and Father

Now, I know I got my strength from my mother. At a very young age, she faithfully went to the mosque to learn the holy book, the Quran. Then at the age of ten or eleven years old, she stopped going to the mosque, because according to the Afghan traditions and religion, she could not go outside her home alone. It was time for her to learn how to cook, clean and do chores at home in preparation for marriage.

At the age of fifteen, she married her cousin, whose name was Akbar. This was (and still is) very common in "traditional" arranged marriages in Afghanistan. Usually cousins and second cousins marry each other, as chosen by their parents. In our culture, this is to make sure that the children are safe, with a good spouse that the family already knows.

Mami worked very hard around the house after she got married, and she also took care of her in-laws who lived in the same house. After five miscarriages, she finally gave birth to her first child. Those losses were hard for her, and she felt rewarded when my sister Pari was born. Then she gave birth to three boys and three girls. Her children were born every 16-18 months, according to Afghan culture.

I was the eighth child, born after my sister, Zaybah. She lost her first son to pneumonia at age one and her second child, a daughter named Asfia, was only ten years old when she died tragically.

Asfia was at my grandfather's house playing up on the roof with other kids and accidentally fell off the roof and died. This broke my mother's heart. She always said, "Asfia was a very smart and beautiful girl." Even after many years, the hole that she left in my mother's heart never seemed to heal.

My dad was in the military, and each morning my mom made sure his shoes were shined, his uniform was clean and pressed, and that all of his medals were polished and in perfect alignment. My dad was tall, had olive-colored skin, dark brown eyes and hair, and broad shoulders. He always looked very handsome and powerful. People everywhere recognized his authority and power just by the sight of him. At home, he was very kind and gentle toward his family. He helped my mom raise us, which was not very common in our culture. My mom used to tell us that whenever we were sick he would rock us to sleep at night.

My father was the only son in his family who actually finished high school. He left home in his late twenties, and joined the military. When my parents first married, they lived in a small town about ten miles from the city of Kabul, the capital of Afghanistan. But since my dad's military base was in Kabul, they moved to the city as soon as my mother was pregnant with her fourth child.

My dad studied medicine and practiced surgery in the army. He treated the entire family, giving us injections when they were needed. He even treated relatives and neighbors at no charge, never asking for anything in return.

Every morning, before my father left for work, all of the kids would gather around him to wish him a good day. He would then ask each one of us, "What do you want me to bring you when I come home?" We always wanted some thing or another, usually candy, a notebook, a pencil or a pair of shoes. It was like a game, a way for each one of us to express ourselves and have a few minutes to laugh with him.

When it was my turn (I must have been about four and a half years old), it was difficult for me to get the words out for what I wanted. I was a loner and kind of quiet, always sitting in the background. I had some kind of speech impediment, and would get nervous trying to speak. All I could say was, "aaaaaah," then I was able to say, *"Bu bu"* (Mom). We would go around in a circle like this three times, because my dad was trying to get me to speak. But by the third time, I would be silent. Then everyone would start laughing. Their laughter was hard for me to accept. They would call me the "mute one," and they thought it was cute.

Even so, I knew my parents loved me, and they acted as if nothing was wrong with me. In private, though, they were very concerned. Sometimes, I would hear them talking about me, and my limited ability to speak at four and a half years old.

Some of my relatives told them, "If you feed her bread from seven Hindu homes she might be able to speak." My dad did not believe in that kind of talk, but my mom was willing to try anything. I don't remember if she really tried it, but knowing my mom's love for me, I'm sure that she did.

My speech impediment suddenly resolved itself when I turned five, and then I could not stop talking. I became a chatterbox and made up for lost time. I was very loud and did not like the teasing anymore, and I would scream whenever my brothers or sisters picked on me.

When I was six years old, I started the first grade with my sister Zaybah, who is eighteen months older than I am. The age requirement for first grade was seven, but my dad knew I was ready; so he insisted that I go, too. We wore the school uniform, which our mother made. It was a long-sleeved dress made of black, cotton fabric that fell below our knees. We covered our heads with a white cotton scarf and wore thick, black stockings to cover our legs. Mother also made our book bags, out of shiny neon-pink plastic, with a zipper along the topside.

My oldest sister Pari used to take us to school every afternoon. She was ten years older than me, and seemed so mature, because she had already completed her elementary school education. She was already wearing the *chaderi*, because our parents told her to. But the other kids made fun of her.

One day, when Pari was about thirteen, one of my father's relatives told him, "You should just let Pari stay home. I heard that my neighbor's high school age daughter is developing 'thoughts of her own.' She's not listening to her parents anymore." This put fear into my dad's heart that the same attitude would develop in Pari. He sat her down and informed her that it was now time for her to stay home and help around the house. Pari now needed to take care of her siblings until she got married. She accepted it, and helped my mom keep my three rambunctious brothers in line.

Amir was the oldest, and then came Zaman and Aman. Because they were born so close together, they played with each other constantly. They were not only brothers, but also best friends. They made and sold kites together, and flew them whenever they had the chance. They also had pigeons, which they caught and raised.

Amir and Zaman picked on Aman constantly. The two oldest had Aman do all their errands, including the menial chores such as starching strings for the kites with his bare hands. The starch was abrasive and Aman had cuts all over his hands and also his feet from not wearing shoes. They were always wrestling and teasing each other, as boys tend to do. Pari would help break up the commotion and get them to calm down. If her efforts weren't successful, my mom would have to stop in the middle of cooking or cleaning to stop the fighting by running them out of the house with a broom.

~~~

My mother, along with most Afghan women, worked very hard during the day. She spent her time baking long flat bread in the *tandoor* – a wood-burning oven made of clay and cement, and dug deep into the ground. The *tandoor* was located in a little room outside the main living area. She started her day early in the morning, making the bread dough. Then she would get breakfast ready and make sure all the kids ate and went to school on time. The older kids went to school in the mornings, while the younger ones (Zaybah and I) went in the afternoons. Mom would feed everyone lunch either before or after school. Sometimes my father would come home for lunch too, which was always a treat.

Then Mom had to think about dinner. Planning our meals was not an easy task, because my dad bought bulk dry food on a monthly basis from a wholesale shop – rice, flour, sugar, tea, cooking oil, seasonings, beans, detergent, and other necessities. He bought fresh veggies, fruit, fresh meat and other such perishables daily.

Mom had to be very frugal and make sure the supplies lasted for an entire month. If she did not do this, her husband was not going to be happy. And, he couldn't buy more supplies until he was paid. So, somehow, she needed to make sure it lasted. This was her job and she did it extremely well.

Most of the time she had to wait for my dad or my brothers

to get her something. It was difficult to see her so dependent. Occasionally, Mom would put on her *chaderi* and go out and get supplies. But since everyone used only cash, if she didn't have any, she would have to ask the vendor for credit, and my dad would pay him later in the week.

If all of this were not enough, she had to keep the house clean, wash the clothes, and make clothes for all of us. Mom was like a well-oiled machine that never failed. She did not work outside the house, because she had more than enough to do at home.

Mom was the sewing expert, and sometimes she even made wedding dresses for our relatives. Because of this, she kept up with all of the family news – weddings, engagement parties, babies, deaths, and so on, and usually knew what was going on in the family before anyone else did. It was her responsibility to know what was going on and to keep the right people informed.

All our relatives lived in Shewakey or Benehisar, villages to the south of Kabul, where my mom and dad grew up. We didn't have phones, so if a wedding or some family event was planned, the family would send someone to spread the news a week or two ahead of time.

If it was a wedding, a group of three or four women would go from home to home. This was called *khabary*, or "giving the good news." At every home they would be given candy or money or some sort of treat in exchange for the news. During the hot weather, this was really a chore, especially for the women who wore *chaderi*s. At the end of the day, one woman in the group divided up all the treats among the women.

If it was not good news, such as a death in the family, they would send men. This was called, "giving the bad news," or *khabar*. However, this was the 1960s, and most modern people living in the city of Kabul announced their family's deaths on the radio.

My mother was used to a big family, because she had two brothers, three sisters, two half brothers and a half sister. She was the oldest and was raised to be very respectful of her brothers and the rest of her family. She grew up in Shewakee, 15-20 miles from the city of Kabul. Her father had a farm and raised animals.

My father's father was a prominent mayor (*malik*) of the nearby town of Benehisar. He married a second wife after his first wife passed away. He had my father and three girls with his first wife, and then three sons and two girls with his second wife. His first wife was my mom's aunt. It was common at the time in Afghanistan for men to have two to four wives at the same time. In fact, it is still common to have at least two wives in some parts of the country today, especially if the first wife or second wife can't have children (sons, in particular).

~~~

In the late 60s, Kabul was still very liberalized, as it had been since the time of King Amanullah Khan. Women were wearing mini skirts and dark shades, had big hairdos, and schoolgirls rode bicycles. It had old world and new world people living in it.

Share-now was the area of Kabul that was most modern, and we lived near there. But our relatives were from villages, and we were more conservative. We wore skirts and short sleeves, but not the *chaderi*s that covered women from head to toe, like a tent. When our aunts and uncles came to visit our home, they would criticize us for not dressing properly, because we didn't cover our heads. So, when our uncles came over, we would grab a scarf and drape it over our heads, just to please them. But generally, after we finished grade school, we never wore headscarves.

Our relatives from the villages continued to visit over the years and go shopping in this modern society. My mother made sure the extended family was treated well. She made their clothes and took brides to beauty shops for special hairdos on their wedding day. My father took the family to concerts, to the circus, and to see fireworks during *Jashin Istiklal* or Independence Festival. *Jashin Istiklal* was celebrated every year for a week, starting on August 19th, when thousands of people commemorated Afghanistan's independence from British rule. The whole city of Kabul used to light up, especially around the stadium and near Kabul *Nendari* theater. On the main streets of Kabul, there were military parades during the day. Boys and girls, elementary school to high school ages, marched in bands and performed traditional folk music and *Attan*, the national Afghan dance. At night, hundreds of thousands of people poured into the city and went to famous singers' concerts and circus shows.

We went to see pop singers such as Ahmad Zahir, Ahmed Wali, and Angoma. Each concert had an area that was decorated with lights near waterfalls, with beautiful trees and flowers. We sat on chairs and watched them perform all the songs that we had listened to on the radio. It was nice to put a face to those songs.

We drank Coke and orange Fanta, ate watermelon, and appetizers like Sambosa and Bolany (fried wraps with potatoes, onions and spices or leeks inside). Those days were so amazing. I still can taste them to this day.

Then at night, we watched fireworks near the stadium. If we were at home, we used to spread out a rug, sit on top of our flat roofs, and watch the fireworks from there. Most of our aunts, uncles, and cousins would come to our house, and my dad would take all of them to see the shows and fireworks, too.

I remember an acrobatic show my dad took us to that was performed by a Russian group. They were doing stunts on a wire cable up in the air; it was unbelievable. A Russian woman was wearing a glittery red, skimpy outfit, and a man was throwing her up in the air and catching her back up on that wire. I'll never forget that moment. It was magical.

There were merchants everywhere selling handmade products, fruits, vegetables, and kabobs and ice cream and non-alcoholic drinks. The best part was that we had no school for the whole week. It was a nationwide celebration. Those times are gone forever.

~~~

Dad used to take us to all the famous parks, such as Paghman Gardens and the presidential gardens, and to Istalef, a beautiful village in the mountains. We went to Kariz-e mir, a king's palace, for picnics, and also to the man-made Lake Kharga. He even took us inside Darul Aman Palace, which was built for King Amanullah Khan and his queen, Soraya. The public couldn't normally go inside – only military personnel. The palace has been destroyed, and so have the beautiful gardens.

My father had two military aids who lived with us, in a small house in the yard, away from the main family area. They helped with yard work, cut wood for the *tandoor* and the woodstove, and sometimes cared for the sheep and goats that we kept for dairy products in the summertime and meat in the wintertime. Uneducated aides stayed with us for two years as part of their service, but educated aids stayed on the base, and did not serve in people's homes.

We had a well, but sometimes the water would dry up, or the water would become nasty and muddy. At those times, they would bring fresh, clean water for cooking and cleaning from a water pump a couple blocks away.

Dad was a very calm and sophisticated man who everyone wanted to be around. Occasionally, he would bring musicians home in the middle of the afternoon, just for entertainment. The musicians were usually a duo: one playing the drums and one playing the harmonium (an accordion-like instrument that you sit on the floor and play). Usually, there was even a young female dancer, barefoot and wearing a traditional afghan dress. The whole family, and sometimes the neighbors, would come and watch them, clapping and enjoying the entertainment.

As the years went by, my father continued to practice medicine in the military, even though he had never formally attended medical school. He was a pharmacy technician, and the type of person who learned everything hands-on. He practiced medicine on his family, relatives, and neighbors and excelled at it.

Sometimes, women who would never dare to show their faces would easily drop their pants to get a shot of antibiotics or vitamin B12 from him. They would keep their faces covered with their big scarves while my dad gave them the injection. And after they left, my dad would make fun of them. "Well, as long as they think I don't know whose butt that is, I guess it's OK."

~~~

In 1997, my half brother was walking on the streets of Kabul. He had returned to Kabul, with his wife and children, after the fighting between the Mujahidin and the Taliban subsided. He was passing piles of debris and half-burned books, papers and magazines. He glanced down, and saw a familiar black and white photo on the ground. He picked it up. It was a photo of my father, the only picture of him that has survived.

My father, the only photo of him that survived the Taliban era.

~ Two ~

My Stepmother

My mother breastfed all of us, but by the time Zaybah was born, her milk dried up. So my parents decided to feed Zaybah formula, and she gained weight and became a chubby little baby. Zaybah especially loved our father, and slept next to him, getting back rubs until she would fall asleep at night. Akbar loved all his children equally, boys and girls alike.

Bu bu-jaan (mother dear) told me that I was born with beautiful olive color skin, dark brown eyes, lots of hair, and chubby, rosy cheeks. When I was born, they also fed me formula, and it seemed to work. Then, they tried adding a little butter to make it richer, like they did for Zaybah. After a couple of days of drinking this rich buttery formula, I developed an allergic reaction. I broke out with a rash and blisters all over my body, and this made my parents very nervous. They stopped the formula and started nondairy products for me, such as pureed rice and bread pudding. As a result of this, I lost a lot of weight and turned to all skin and bone. My father treated me with penicillin injections for the blisters. I survived all of that, and little by little, started gaining weight. I never seemed to totally recover though, because I was always thin and clothes did not fit me right. From the earliest times that I can remember, my siblings were constantly teasing me for being so skinny and weak.

~~~

My mother's life began to get very busy and complicated just before I was born. My father was too busy at work to help her anymore. Then all of a sudden, he decided to take another wife.

One of Dad's military aides was from a village called Nejrab in the northern part of Afghanistan. He offered my dad his sister to marry for a small sum of money. She was probably sixteen or seventeen years old. This was (and still is) a very common practice in those parts of the country. My dad kept saying, "No, I don't need to marry another wife." But the aide wanted my dad to marry his sister. So he went to my dad's father, and said, "Your son wants to marry my sister. And they already had the *nekah*." *Nekah* is the ceremony that occurs when there is an agreement to marry.

My grandfather came to our house and confronted my dad.

"You're destroying our family name!" he said. "You *nekah* someone, and you don't marry her?"

My dad said, "No, I did not *nekah*." But my grandfather insisted, telling my dad that he should marry this girl.

My grandfather had never been happy with his son for marrying my mother and moving to the city. And now, he had an opportunity for revenge. My mom got upset and told my grandfather to leave.

By this time, rumors had spread that my father had agreed to marry the aide's sister. My mom wanted to avoid anything that could shame the family name, so she talked it over with my dad. She told him to go ahead and marry the girl.

Before she knew it, this other woman named Zewar was in our home, tripping all over things. My mother worked hard to orient her to the house and chores. She even loaned this woman her own *chaderi*, because in the villages people didn't wear *chaderi*s. She taught her how to walk, how to talk, and how to eat like a civilized person. After all, this woman was not used to city life, and my mom did not want her to be made fun of when she went into public places and to our relatives' homes. Zewar was about twenty years younger than my father, and it truly bothered my mom, but she did what she had to in order to make it work.

The extended family on my father's side began treating his new wife better than my mom, and my mom became very depressed after Dad married Zewar. My dad's sisters were trying to tear the family apart. My mom was more liberated than they were, and they had always disliked the fact that my mom sent her kids to school.

Fortunately, Zewar learned quickly and helped around the house. She even took care of Zaybah and me. But again, my sister Zaybah had the worst of it of anyone in the house. Out of the clear blue sky, she had to share her father with this strange woman, and eventually lost her dad to Zewar completely. Zaybah went into an even deeper depression than my mom.

At the same time, my mom and dad's youngest daughter, Rona, was born. Then Zewar got pregnant with her first child. Suddenly, it appeared that it was Zewar's turn to have babies. She wanted to have as many children as *Mami*, and this is where the rivalry started. Zewar did not want to be less of a woman, so she became competitive with my mom.

I was about two years old when Zewar's first daughter, Nazeefa, was born. She was beautiful, with light skin like her mother, and dark brown eyes and hair like her father. Zewar had a lot of breast milk, so she nursed Nazeefa and Rona at the same time. At least now, mom didn't need to worry about feeding Rona. Zewar was short in stature and quick on her feet. She knew how to make everyone like her. But deep down, she knew that she would eventually turn Akbar against my mother and her children.

By now, the big house was getting too small for everyone. The boys were sleeping in one room with Pari, because she kept them in line. Mom slept with us three younger daughters in the same room, along with Zewar and her child Nazeefa, on the opposite side of the room. This room was used as a family room during the day, and then as a dining room during mealtime, and our bedroom at night. We all slept on long, handmade cushions mother had made. My father took turns sleeping with each wife.

The fighting got worse after Zewar had more children. In the middle of the night, Zewar would purposely say something to upset my mother. Then it escalated to fighting and screaming that would wake up all the kids, even the boys in the other room. Then the younger kids would start crying, and my dad didn't know what to do.

I would start to panic, and pray that everything would calm down, so we could go back to sleep. I dreaded the nights. Sometimes, the fighting got so bad that *Bu bu-jaan* and her children would get kicked out of the main room. Some nights, my mom and us kids would just go and hide in a little room in the back, and everyone would stay quiet for a little bit. We eventually had to come together for meals and cleaning.

As a result, and in an effort to keep some dignity, my mother moved into a separate bedroom with all of her children. We lived like that for about ten years.

Elementary School

Zaybah and I attended an elementary school three miles from our home. I was afraid of going to school, but I felt secure as long as my older sister, Pari, stayed in the back of the classroom with me. As soon as Pari left the room, Zaybah and I would run after her.

My first grade teacher was a 65-year-old, 5-foot tall man with a long white beard, who was very strict and stern looking. He carried a knife in his pocket so that he could sharpen our bamboo pens that we dipped into the inkwells. The children were not allowed to talk in the classroom, or he would beat their little hands with a wooden stick and say, "This is your punishment!" Every afternoon, before he started class, he prayed at his desk.

During the school year, Zaybah and I waited for our father at the Mosque Eid-gah so that he could give us a ride home on his bicycle. We had to walk about a quarter of a mile from school and wait at the busiest intersection in Kabul, near the stadium, where thousands of people were walking around. Some days he would get off work late, so the policeman guiding traffic at the intersection would tease Zaybah and me. "Your father is not coming," he would say. That scared me to death. But Zaybah knew better, and she would tell him, "Our father would never forget about us." Of course, he would show up just minutes later and take his little girls home.

I rode up front and Zaybah rode on the back of the bike. My father sang folk songs throughout the bumpy ride home on the gravel roads. One of his favorites was, *"Allah Shakoko-jaan,"* a love song about a girl from Kandahar. He sang, "I sacrifice for your almond-shaped eyes and your pearly lips and teeth. Come in so we can sit together knee to knee." His second favorite song was, *"Nazanine amdameman delbareman, nazy amdameman,"* meaning, "Nazanine is my breath and my heart." His heart was always so full of life and he shared it with us.

One day, in the middle of the hot sun, we were walking toward the intersection from school. We passed through a secluded area, and an older man in his 30s started chasing us. He kept yelling at us, wanting us to stop and "talk" with him. We knew something was wrong, and we ran like the wind and kept running until we arrived at the intersection. We were relieved to see the policeman, because he knew our father. I was trembling and scared, and Zaybah comforted me. Fortunately for us, we never saw that man again.

My mother always told us to look down while we walked to school. "Don't look around. And don't look at or talk to men," she said. We were told to cover ourselves and not to show our skin or hair. We were not supposed to get too close to male family members – in fact we weren't even supposed to talk to our cousins. But at home, it was OK to talk with our brothers, and we could talk with our uncles, as long as we were covered.

I passed the first grade with the highest score in the classroom. As I began second grade, I realized that I was a big girl now, and I looked forward to studying when I arrived home from school. Zaybah was in the same class with me, so that made it all the more fun. We were best friends and loved to be together. We slept in the same room, took baths together, and played dolls together. We were like twins. Only, Zaybah had to sit in the third row with not so bright kids. Sometimes she would have to stand on the chair with some of her classmates as a punishment for not doing her homework.

We were taught religion by an older woman, who wanted everyone to recite the Quran in Arabic. If we did not, she would have everyone stand up and put their hands out for her to beat them with a wooden stick.

The middle row was for intermediate level students. I always sat in the first row because I was such a good student. The teacher loved me and tormented Zaybah by saying, "Your sister is smarter. Why can't you be like her?" I felt bad for Zaybah, and I did not want to hurt her, because she was my protector. Unfortunately, Zaybah had to repeat the second grade, and I went on to third grade.

~ Three ~

Paktia

While I was in the third grade, my father was transferred to Paktia, a province in the South of Afghanistan, very close to Pakistan. I was so happy about that, because we moved to a bigger house, and I wouldn't have my mean Quran teacher anymore.

But living in the province was not so great for us city people. We didn't have any relatives there, and there were more restrictions for women: we couldn't go out in public without a male figure, and we needed to be covered at all times.

There wasn't as much to do for us kids who were used to city life. The weather was tortuously cold, and it snowed all the time. My three brothers were now teenagers and were always misbehaving. They were fighting all the time, and they caused a lot of chaos in our home. But they were happy when they were raising their pigeons and making their kites.

Zaybah, Rona and I, along with my half sisters, Nazeefa and Rozy, continued our schooling. We all wore the same kind of black, cotton dresses and white, thin cotton scarves. We walked about one mile to school each day with Pari.

At home, after school, we played together with dolls that my mom made for us. They were stuffed with cotton balls and had hair made of yarn. We had log dollhouses outside in the yard, which we made ourselves from wooden logs just lying around. Sometimes the neighbor's girls joined us, and we cooked rice in the wood-burning pit and played all day long. At night, Pari made us come inside to eat dinner.

Sometimes, I used to get upset over things and cry a lot. It seemed that no one was paying attention to me but Pari. She would hug me and say, "Don't cry, it will make you sick and weak. You're a big girl, don't cry," and take me inside. My mom was too busy taking care of everything, and did not have much time to spend with each individual child.

One day, when I was still very young, she heard me talking with a bunch of kids. I said, "I do not have a mother." Obviously, this hurt her feelings very much. She called to me, and as I went toward her, I saw tears rolling down her face. Then she hugged and kissed me saying, "I am your mother, and I love you very much."

I liked singing, so one day when I was around ten years old, I started singing outside in the yard. My youngest brother, Aman said, "Stop it! Don't sing! All the neighbors are going to hear you." It was not considered proper for a good girl to sing. I didn't listen to him and kept singing. Aman gave me a hard slap across my face. That was enough to keep me from singing but not from crying. Pari had to comfort me and scold Aman.

At school, we learned *Pashto* as our second language. *Pashto* was the local language in Paktia, and all the classes were taught in *Pashto*. I learned very quickly, and the principal was very happy to have me as a top student in third grade.

Eventually, Pari was offered a teaching position at the small elementary, middle and high school. She was about nineteen years old and had only graduated elementary school, but she was very good at teaching first and second grades. People respected her in the community, and the principal was happy to have Pari as a teacher at the school.

One day, my dad's military aides were escorting us to school, and they asked if they could carry our bags as a sign of respect to my father. All the other military kids were having it done for them, and they did not dare upset my dad. Pari told them, "Leave us alone, because it is not proper for young girls to walk with strangers on the same road." Since they were not family, they were considered strangers. My other sisters and I, on the other hand, wanted them to carry our bags, but we had to respect our older sister's decision.

I went to a girls' school, mostly for daughters of military families, since local families didn't usually send their girls to school. The school was big, with a large garden and greenhouse. The greenhouse did not have any plants inside it, although there were lots of plants and flowers outside. It was used during the rainy season and cold weather, mainly for many small classrooms, each one separated by curtains. Sometimes it got very noisy inside, and we had to keep really quiet.

There were no classes during the wintertime, when the snow made it too difficult for children to get to school and stay warm, because there was no heating system. During the summertime, classes were held in the garden, under the big, old trees that were part of the Provincial General's house. He lived on the other side of the courtyard with his two wives and his six or seven kids. His daughters attended the same school as we did. He had gardeners who took care of the large garden, and also a chef and servants. There were apple, peach, apricot and cherry trees in the garden, but no one was allowed to touch them.

One day, when the principal was not around, all the kids got a hold of the ripe cherries and ate as many as they could. I, on the other hand, saved mine to take home and share them with my family. The other kids told on me. The school principal made me take the cherries out of my bag in front of the class and give them to him. I was very embarrassed to be punished in front of my classmates. After that, I hated the school principal and did not trust him again.

~~~

At this point, my father was doing well in the military and became very sought-after for advice and consultation. He was ranked as a *Kandakmeshir*, or colonel. There were military gatherings every Friday, which was the only day off during the week. In Afghanistan, the weekend starts on Thursday afternoon and lasts until Saturday morning.

My father was invited on a regular basis to the home of the village's *malik* (mayor), and he would take both of his wives and all of his children with him. There, we were treated like royalty. During these visits, the men of the village stayed with the men of the family, and the women took care of everything – preparing the meals, serving, and even rubbing the backs and feet of the guests. The provincial people did not speak the native language of city people, which is *Dari* (a very close cousin to the Persian language of Farsi). Most of these southern and eastern country people spoke *Pashto*; but we all got along well, despite the communication barriers.

It turned out that the Provincial General (who was my dad's superior) was not happy with my father gaining all this popularity. After one of these long weekend trips, we came back home. We thought it was just a normal Saturday morning, and we all went to school and my dad went to work.

Everyone was surprised to see us back at school. Apparently, they were all aware of my father's status. He was told (without any warning) that he had two options: take an early retirement, or be fired. That was a big blow to the family. My father came home, and told us the news.

My mother was crying, "What are we going to do now?" She got upset and was hitting her arms and her legs, which she often did when she was under stress. I think she felt she had the weight of the world on her shoulders. We felt very bad for our father that day, because he had always been in control, and that was taken away from him. We had no idea where our income was going to come from, and it was in the middle of the school year during summertime. Suddenly, after two and a half years in Paktia, we had to get ready to leave our military home and go back to Kabul.

My family had been raising sheep and goats just like any other military family. The weather was hot, and we could not take the animals with us that we would need for our winter meat. We had to do the butchering earlier than planned, in the fall. Since there was no refrigeration, my parents hung the meat up to dry in a cool room. Unfortunately, because of the heat, the meat spoiled. My mother did not know what else to do but throw it all out. She was upset and she cried for days. Of course, this meant we had to be very frugal for the upcoming winter, especially now that my dad was retired from the military.

~ Four ~

Return to Kabul

We packed everything and went home to Kabul. My father was forced to retire at age fifty-five, ten years earlier than he should have. Now, he was staying home with both wives and all the children. Zewar was still having children, which made things more difficult financially. To fill the vacuum of "what to do," Dad suddenly got involved in everyday meal planning and spending. This was not a picnic for my mom. She now had him around every second of every day to tell her what to do and how to do it. Of course, this led to more fights and disagreements than ever before.

After Dad received his retirement pay-off, my mother encouraged him to open a bicycle shop. He mainly sold parts for bicycles. He liked being his own boss, actually, and sometimes my brothers and half brother worked with him.

Zewar now had four children, and she didn't like to be just a caretaker, having to do all the household chores. She wanted to be independent from my mom and her kids. My brothers were growing up, and they argued with my father constantly. They blamed their unhappiness on my father, for marrying a second wife and ruining their lives.

My parents had a second house next door, which they rented. My brothers suggested to my father that our side of the family move into my dad's second house. They said they would get jobs to support themselves and our family. But my dad said, "That's my house, and the tenants will stay there because I will need that money. Once you guys get a job and get rich, you can have your own houses."

My brothers were only in high school, and Mom kept telling them, "Try to get along with everyone. Wait a little longer, and finish school." Mom wanted them to go to college. They kept insisting on getting jobs instead of finishing their education. But, since Dad wouldn't let them move to the other house and become independent, they had to stay in school.

Around the same time, my father had Pari married off to Zewar's cousin. Her husband had no source of income, so Pari continued living with us, too. Her husband was getting his engineering degree from Russia. He would come home once a year in the summer, spend a month and go back. He did this for six years. Pari soon had two children, who were added to the rest of our family. Zewar now had five children. So, my father finally decided to separate the two wives into different rooms (but still within the same house) where they could take care of their own kids, cook and clean. He bought groceries for both families, but our personal grocery budget was cut into half. My mom had to be even more careful with spending. She started mending and sewing clothes for money just to make ends meet, spending most of her time working over the sewing machine, while Pari helped with the cooking and cleaning.

Winter had arrived and was taking its toll on us in the little room that we lived in. We all slept together on the floor next to each other, just to keep warm. Mom taught us the Quran in Arabic and prayed for our survival. She told us stories about her life as a child.

Then she told us how her in-laws had turned against her after Zewar came along. They were much nicer to Zewar, but tormented my mother and her children. The only reason for this was that Zewar lived a lifestyle that they personally agreed with: she did not let her daughters continue their education past elementary school. Mom told us, "You need to finish your education, go to college, and become independent." She did not want her kids to suffer as much as she did, having to depend on a husband who was no longer there for her.

Out of all of my relatives, my parents (Mariam and Akbar) were the only ones who sent their children to school and college. They knew the importance of a solid education and wanted us to be prepared for life. This never sat well with the rest of the family.

Our only source of income was my Dad's retirement and the monthly rent that he got from his second home. That is, when we had good tenants who paid their rent. Sometimes they would trash our home and creep away in the middle of the night without paying.

One time, the renters got very violent with my dad. They would have killed him had it not been for my mom. The rent was already months late, and when he went there to collect it, the whole family attacked him. My mom came in carrying a long piece of lumber – like a two-by-four – and swung her way through the crowd of people. She found my dad on the floor, where they were beating him up. She brandished her two-by-four and got Dad out of there. Later they tried to say she had injured them, and we were afraid of what they were going to do. But we just stayed home and waited a few days until they finally left.

My Half Siblings

My oldest half sister Nazeefa died at age ten of a bleeding disorder. She bled for a month or two from her nose and mouth. My dad tried to treat her at home with no success. He did not want her to go to the hospital, because he didn't trust hospitals, and thought he could take better care of her at home. The health care system in Afghanistan at that time was unsafe, and I know he was right to feel that way.

When Nazeefa became unresponsive one day, he had a doctor come to the house to see her, but it was too late. The doctor pronounced her dead. Our whole family was devastated, because we all loved Nazeefa so much. Mom loved her like of one her own children – Nazeefa always clung to Mom and us. Nazeefa had a stray, black cat that came every day to visit her and hang out with her all day. Even though no other cats and dogs were allowed in the house, this was the one animal that received special treatment. At the exact time of Nazeefa's death, the cat disappeared. It was like an omen.

There was always something special about Nazeefa. She was a most beautiful girl with dark black hair and eyes, light skin and rosy cheeks. She just seemed to light up any room that she entered. Nazeefa's death was especially hard on me. I couldn't understand how someone so nice and beautiful could die. I cried a lot when no one was watching. She was part of us girls, especially when we played with dolls. We all pretended we were related to famous Afghan singers like Ahmad Zahir and Ahmad Wali and lived a rich life. Sometimes we were the royal family of the King Zahir Shah. We had so much fun. To this day, I still miss her deeply.

Jamal was my oldest half brother, and about six years younger than me. He seemed to follow in Nazeefa's footsteps. He was as close to us as she had been, and he was devastated when his sister died.

The day she died, I came into the room and saw him actually beating on the doctor.

He loved my mother and was extremely kind for a boy in our culture. When I was older, he used to rub my shoulders when I was tired. Though we were close with Jamal, we were not nearly as close to the younger siblings, since our two families were now separated. There seemed to be a lot of jealousy and competition going on among the children for our father's attention and love.

One time, Dad tried to stop an awful fight between my mother and my stepmom. He tied my mother to the big tree in the middle of the yard with a rope. We were looking out the window witnessing this horrible scene, and Pari was trying to calm us down and comfort us. I will never forget that scene as long as I live. That was the only time my dad was physically abusive to my mom, as far as I know.

I can only imagine that my father was overwhelmed and felt pushed over the edge by having two wives, fourteen children, forced early retirement, and the responsibility of supporting two separate households. His tolerance level was getting low, and he was being pulled in sixteen different directions (literally). He could not split himself so many ways. There was no other way for him to deal with things, because according to the culture and customs in Afghanistan, my parents did not believe in divorce. Divorce was considered an embarrassment that would bring shame to the whole family. Finally, he had to choose which wife to live with, and it was not my mom.

My half brothers and sisters acted like the winners, since my dad chose to live with them. We were the "not-so-loved children," and we felt that way, too. We did not feel comfortable seeing my dad or talking to him anymore. He had become a stranger to us. We felt abandoned and betrayed by him because he was no longer with our mother. We could not understand how everything had changed from those happy childhood days, when we used to ride on the back of his bike and listen to the folk songs he sang to us.

~ Five ~

School

I went to fifth grade, and just when I was getting more comfortable with school, I developed tonsillitis. I was always sick with a sore throat and fever and could not breathe at night. My mom used to sit beside me and wake me up whenever my tonsils blocked my airway and I could not breathe. Father kept treating me with antibiotics every day. My skinny buttocks were sore from all the shots. My tonsils got bigger and more inflamed to the point that I could not eat solid food. I could not even read aloud in the classroom, as my throat would get very sore when I did. Once again, I had become the "mute one."

My mother took me to the Mullah, the preacher of the village in which she grew up. He put some kind of herb on the tip of his finger, and reached in the back of my throat and pressed the very swollen and painful tonsils as hard as he could a couple times. It made me gag and made me sick to my stomach. Then he prayed in Arabic for God to heal me. My mom then took me to the holy shrines, and rubbed stones from the shrine on the outside of my throat and prayed for me to get better. Then she put the stones on each of her eyes, kissed them and put them back.

They did everything they could but take me to the doctor, because my father did not trust doctors and hospitals, even after what had happened with my half sister. This went on for about four years. Finally, one day my oldest brother Amir decided that he had a "treatment plan." He himself took me to Ibne Sina hospital, where my cousin Ghulam Mohammed worked. He was a very famous and powerful cardiologist in Kabul. It was a snowy day, one where you could not even see the road. We took two buses to get there. After the buses, we found ourselves walking for another mile on icy roads. I vaguely remember sliding and falling on ice. I was feverish and getting very tired. Amir had to carry me the rest of the way. I was sixteen years old, weighed about eighty pounds, and had absolutely no endurance. They scheduled me for a tonsillectomy a couple of days later.

Amir took me back to the hospital the day of surgery. My dad could not say no to Amir now, because he was the oldest and had actually taken on some authority, due to the fact that my dad lived in the other home. My surgery was done by the senior ENT (ears nose and throat) doctor. I found myself sitting in a chair awake with my mouth open for the procedure. The minute I felt tired and could not open my mouth as wide as the doctor wanted, I saw his fist up in the air, and I heard him say, "I will hit you with this if you cannot keep your mouth open."

It was then that I knew "why" my father would not let me have the surgery until this point. I felt very scared and opened my mouth as wide as I could for the rest of the procedure. After it was done, I saw two golf ball-sized tonsils sitting in a container. The doctor then decided to add insult to injury, telling me, "You can take them home and kabob them, if you really want to," and then he laughed (I didn't think it was funny). I stayed in the hospital for a few days, and there was another girl in my room who had had the same procedure done. An hour after her procedure, she started bleeding all over the place because her sutures separated, and they had to take her back to repair them. I was very uncomfortable moving around and scared from seeing what happened to her, so I stayed on my back until the next morning.

The doctor came to make rounds the next day and laughed at me one more time for not moving (I was actually waiting for permission to get up and move around). Apparently, there was not enough nursing staff to make the rounds on tonsillectomy patients. The next day, my father came to visit me. He brought me a slice of pound cake, dipped it in warm sweet milk, and fed it to me. My second brother, Zaman, came too and he did something that made me feel better than anything else. Since he knew that I actually worried more about my mom's health than my own, he went home to give the good news to my mom. He told her that I was doing well. "She even looks good in the hospital gown," he joked.

I got better. My energy came back slowly and I actually gained some weight for the first time in a long time. I did not get sick as often and had no breathing problems. My health finally started to improve, which was amazing after having been sick for so long.

My biggest problem was yet to come. After recovering for a couple of weeks, I went back to school in the ninth grade. Since my throat was still healing, and I was afraid of hurting it more, I developed a new speech pattern that was not "quite right." I would get anxious, my throat would spasm, and I would strain my throat more and more, to the point that my voice came out from the back of my throat, which was very harsh and unpleasant. Reading out loud in class became even more of a challenge. I avoided speaking at all and panicked each time the teacher called on me. By the time I was done reading, I would feel tired and drained, because of not breathing well and straining my throat. As a result, I would feel dizzy and sweaty, and my chest hurt. It was like a panic attack. I did not know what was happening to me and did not know what to do about it. The other students looked at me strangely, and I felt very embarrassed.

I somehow made it through the ninth and tenth grades, but I never discussed my speech problems or panic attacks with my parents or anyone else in the family. I was so ashamed of being weak and shy. I thought that was my problem and no one could help me. By the time I was in the eleventh grade, I began to panic every time I was asked to read aloud or to come to the front of the classroom to read or write on the board. I had a *Pashto* language teacher, who would call on me to read the previous day's lesson aloud as soon as she walked in the classroom. The very second my name was called, my heart would start pounding hard, and I would start sweating and shaking. My voice would start cracking, and I could not catch my breath. I felt like my body temperature rose 200 degrees, and I was dizzy. I felt like I was having a heart attack every time this happened.

The teacher never said anything about it, never discussed it with me or asked me about what was going on. She just made me do this every time, every day. Maybe deep down, she thought she was helping me to get over my anxiety. Little did she know that she was scarring me for life. After class, some girls would ask me what was wrong. I was embarrassed. "I have a weak heart," I explained. At least that is what it felt like, and I diagnosed my own condition.

Despite the challenge of speaking in front of my classmates, I still had the second highest grade in the classroom. I thought my grades could have been higher yet had it not been for the shyness and fear. I sat in the back of the classroom and did not participate much. I loved exam days and would look forward to them, because I did not have to read aloud or speak in front of the class. I would take the test, get the highest score, go home and get ready for the next day's test, which did not take me long. I would memorize the whole subject matter in two or three hours. That is all we had to do – memorize the whole book. My sister, Zaybah, on the other hand, would pace the yard, circling it a million times, reading and studying up to the very last second just to pass.

~~~

I finished twelfth grade at the new Arianna High School for girls, right across from the Nejat High School for boys. My classmates were into having secret boyfriends and going places, but I did not have to worry about that. After all, I was not the typical light-skinned, full-figured Afghan girl. Whenever I walked to the bus stop or walked home, boys would make comments about my dark skin, calling me "*siagak*," which means black. I felt ugly all the time. I was skinny as a stick, and I didn't think I had any sense of fashion.

I was always embarrassed when I was with a group of my classmates, too shy to talk to anyone in my class, even though it was an all girls' school. I always had one or two friends that would sit close to me in class. I felt they were only my friends because they felt sorry for me, since I did not talk to anyone else.

I had to take two buses to school, and my father would only give me bus fare for one bus, so I had to walk another 3-4 miles to get to or from school. During my senior year, my friend Treena and I rode the bus together sometimes. She lived close to us, and I knew her family. Treena always told me, "I will read aloud for you anytime in class, since you don't like to." Once, when I had some kind of infection on my heel, I could not walk for a couple of weeks, and had to stay home. Treena and her mother came to visit me. That is when I knew that she was a true friend and not just someone who felt sorry for me.

During this time, there were lots of political riots going on. Zahir Shah was the king, and just before his cousin came and took over, students were protesting on the street. One group was called Parcham, and another was "*khalque*," meaning, "The People." Later when the Russians came, this became the Communist Party. I wasn't part of any of that. After school, I just wanted to come home.

After I graduated from high school, I took the entrance exam to enroll in Kabul University, the only university in Afghanistan. I did not get in, and did not even get my scores back for some reason. It seemed like the only people who actually got in to college were kids who had someone in their family with connections – if they knew someone of a high rank in the military, or if they were related to someone at the university. I was very disappointed, and I did not know what to do.

I did not want to stay home or, even worse, be married off to a cousin by my family. I could not even get an office job, because my family would not allow it. They did not think office jobs were for good girls, since these women "worked with men." We had to either become a teacher or a nurse to work outside the home, and there was no other option. So my mom took Zaybah and me to nursing school to enroll us. She was braver than we were, and had more faith in us then we had ourselves. Here we were, new high school graduates, and could not even enroll ourselves in nursing school. She liked this profession, because she had seen the nurses at the hospital and was very impressed by their hard work and the importance of their work. This is why she wanted us to become nurses.

In Afghanistan the university was free then, and they even

paid a small amount of money to students once they entered the program they had chosen. The monthly allowance helped us pay for some expenses, like books. Zaybah and I liked the nursing program and went every day. We were in separate classes. I loved the clinical classes because we worked with the patients. I was still very shy and had problems reading in the classroom, which I avoided as much as I could. One of my favorite teachers got upset with me for not wanting to read aloud when she asked me to read. She reported me to my homeroom teacher. My homeroom teacher started yelling at me.

I could not explain to anyone why I did not want to read out loud. That was the worst part of any experience I ever had during my education. We did not have a counselor I could talk to, and I just had to put it out of my mind and endure it. It was all my weakness and problem, and I told myself, I just have to live with it. But somehow, I never let it stop me from continuing my education. I had no other options, because family life was not happy and I had no one else to turn to. I was stuck and determined not to fail. Deep down, I knew continuing my education was the right thing to do. But there were times at this point when I wished that I was really mute – like when I was young – because at least then, I would have an excuse.

I began to feel sorry for myself. But then, out of the blue, I would look at my mother, and see how brave and strong she was. I would think about how she never went to school. She grew up on a farm and none of her siblings went to school, except the youngest brother who went into the military and became very successful. I would reflect on the fact that, even though she didn't have a formal education, *Mami* was still the most articulate, organized, intelligent and social person in the family.

After thinking about all of these things, I would pull myself out of my pity party and press onward.

~ Six ~

Rona

My youngest sister, Rona, was growing up fast and developing into a young woman by the age of twelve. Rona was very pretty, and carried herself well. She was very fashion-conscious, and the minute she left the house on the way to school, she took off her plain, white cotton headscarf and hid it in her bag. She would then fold her skirt at the top to make it into a miniskirt, and she'd make her stockings look thinner than ours, by stretching them until they were sheer.

Furthermore, she wouldn't listen to Zaybah or me about following the rules. She had the highest grade in her class, and appeared very confident and intelligent at school. So my uncle came and asked my mom to give Rona to his son as his wife. At first, Mom was very reluctant and said "no" to her brother, because Rona was too young and needed to finish her schooling. Then, my mom's other brother, the colonel Mohamad Khan, went to my dad's bicycle shop and proposed the arrangement. My father didn't say anything and told him that they would discuss it later since he was busy.

My uncle came back home to my mom, and said that my dad agreed to the proposal. He passed candy around to everyone to announce the engagement. My mom was shocked that my dad would agree to such a thing. But out of respect for her brother, she didn't question him, and was silent.

Before she knew it, the news of Rona and my cousin's engagement spread everywhere and became official.

When my dad came home, he was furious with my mom for believing her brother. He told her, "I did not approve the engagement!" Now, everyone was angry with my mom for not questioning her brother. My dad, my brothers, and all of us blamed her for the arrangement. It was too late now for my mom to explain or change the decision that was made by my uncle, because it would have been disrespectful. That was the painful part for her, and I don't think she ever forgave herself.

My brothers and I did not want to see our sister get married at such a young age. My uncle asked Rona if she wanted to get married, to see how she felt about it (she was only fourteen years old). She was scared and didn't know what to say. They told my mom that according to them, "If a girl does not verbalize anything, it means the answer is 'yes.'" We all kept telling her, "Say no." But Rona was too young to understand what it all meant. Suddenly she was engaged, and never did finish her grade school education. My uncles said she'd be home schooled, but that never happened.

On the other hand, my stepmother Zewar believed that fourteen was a good age for girls to get married. In fact, she married off her daughters – my half sisters – at the age of fourteen or fifteen to their cousins. She did not let them go to school, because this was the normal practice of families who came from the villages.

So, Rona married our uneducated cousin, who was a few years older than she was, and she was happy for a little while because she got new clothes, a wedding and all the attention that came with that.

Then, suddenly after the wedding, she became very unhappy. We knew, because every time Rona came to visit, she did not want to go back home to her husband. We had to talk her into going back with him each time. She would leave crying, "I don't want to go home!" That was because she lived with her in-laws and they made her do the housework, sweep the floors, wash clothes with her bare hands, and clean up after the animals.

Her mother-in-law baked bread in the *tandoor*, and cooked lamb soup every day for her husband. Her father-in-law would only eat his wife's food. My uncle was very handsome, and loved his wife's cooking, but did not love his wife. He spoke of her as if she were the ugliest person in the world. Her arms were long and tough from cooking all day. She smoked the hookah and always had a terrible cough. Since they lived in the village, Rona had to give up her fashion sense and was made to wear a *chaderi*. Her husband walked a distance ahead of her on the street, because that was the custom. It was shameful to be "next" to a woman in public.

Everyone blamed my mom for letting Rona get married to her cousin. My brothers Amir and Zaman were especially upset because they didn't think he was good enough for Rona, and no one listened to their opinions. Although Amir went to Rona's new home to educate her, all of her neighbors and relatives had to gossip about it, saying, "She's married now. There's no reason to continue her studies. She needs to focus on her marriage and take care of her old in-laws and give them grandchildren before they die."

The guilt was horrible for my mom. Rona miscarried a few times, but eventually she gave birth to a little girl when she was sixteen years old. She had a son a year later, and then a child every year after that, because it was against tradition to use birth control.

~ Seven ~

Nursing School

By now, our home was overcrowded with Pari's two children and Rona, who visited often with her children. There were seventeen people sharing a four-room house, with two rooms for us and two for Zewar and her kids. My mom finally got permission from my father to move us into Dad's second house. She could not take any of her furniture, because Dad wouldn't let her. So she had to start all over again. During the first few nights, all we had were our sleeping mats, pillows and comforters. But we were very happy to be on our own, because that meant there was less fighting going on between *Mami* and Zewar.

In addition to losing her furnished house, Mom felt abandoned by my dad. She did not like losing her husband to Zewar. She felt defeated, but tried to be strong for us and make the best out of a difficult situation.

It was the mid 1970s, and my brothers, Amir and Zaman, were going to college. The country was being run by Zahir Shah's cousin Daoud Khan, and he was the King now. Life was peaceful and normal. There were foreign agencies working alongside Afghans in health care and education everywhere, without any fear.

They were developing new programs for students and health care workers like Zaybah and me.

Amir and Zaman saved the little allowance that the university gave them for their future. They rode their bicycles to school, and Mom continued to pack their lunches. My younger brother, Aman, was still in high school. He became the mediator between the older brothers and our father when Amir and Zaman would get into arguments with Father about house rules, politics, religion, and even card games. They wanted to be the "true" men of the house, even going so far as to throw my stepmom out of her room one day when my dad was not home because Pari and my stepmom started to fight. They were very proud of themselves, but only for a while, because when Father heard about this, he became furious with Amir and Zaman. My brothers said, "We had to do it, to stop the arguments." But my father made them apologize to our stepmom and to promise never to exhibit their authority over her again.

During this time, I was enrolled in nursing school and receiving good grades. I still panicked when I had to read aloud, but was able to cover it up and did better over time, and some of my teachers commended my good grades. I felt it was time to figure out why I continued to have panic attacks. I went to the doctor, and he examined me and did an EKG. Everything came back normal. I secretly wished they would find something wrong with me so I could get treatment for the attacks. One time, on my labor and delivery rotation in nursing school, I became anxious when the head nurse told me to give an injection to a patient. I was holding the syringe and dropped the glass syringe onto the concrete floor, and it broke into pieces. She yelled at me and told me that I would have to pay for the broken syringe.

Another time, I was doing a presentation on the cardiovascular system in an auditorium. I had my presentation ready, with illustrations of the heart, arteries and veins drawn beautifully on the board with different colored chalk. All of the senior classes gathered after lunch for the presentation (about 200 people). When I went in front of the auditorium and stood there to speak, I froze, and my words would not come out of my mouth. When I did start talking, my voice was shaking and I kept losing track. My teacher was very disappointed with me. After all, I was the smartest one in the class. Once again, I was very embarrassed, and went home kicking myself for being panicky. I arrived at home very upset, feeling sick to my stomach, and did not know what to do. I could not talk to my family, for I did not think they would understand me. I thought they would just make fun of me.

I could not even talk to Zaybah, because she was too busy struggling with her studies. At least she wasn't shy and she was able to speak her mind. She formed many friendships at nursing school, but she never knew how bad I felt about her struggling to learn, and she never knew about my panic attacks. In fact, I think she was jealous of my intelligence and ability to grasp the information more quickly than she could.

After three years in nursing school, our graduation day was approaching. The day before graduation, all of us girls got together to try to look our best. We waxed our legs for the first time in our lives. We were crying from pain every time we had to peel the wax off, and we were laughing at the same time. The next day we went to the hairdressers, and had our hair done for the first time in our lives. We all looked pretty with our blue nursing dresses and starched white caps, as we rode in a cab to our graduation, laughing and joking. We were having so much fun, when all of a sudden, in the middle of all of the excitement, I started panicking. My heart started racing. I was feeling hot, sweaty and shaky and I couldn't breathe.

My thoughts turned to death, and I suddenly wanted to end my life, right there. I almost tried to open the door during the ride to jump out; then I couldn't do it. I realized that I had too much to live for. So, I took a deep breath and said to myself, I couldn't do this to my mother. She has suffered enough, and in my heart, I knew that I was better than that, and it was really not the right solution. I still loved life in spite of everything that I went through. But I didn't know what else to do. My panic attacks continued to get worse. Nobody understood, nor could I confide in anyone.

I felt so embarrassed, that I began to deal with these episodes by just avoiding situations. I began to realize that this was happening anytime there was a big change in my life. I thought I was the only person in the world who had this kind of problem, and there was nothing anyone could do about it. Somehow, though, I convinced myself to go on, as I was not a quitter.

Zaybah and I graduated with our nurse-midwifery diplomas. I thanked God for sustaining us during such a difficult time in our lives.

~~~

Zaybah went to work in a hospital as a registered nurse on the medical-surgical floor and made many more friends. She was very happy because she didn't have to study anymore. She made money and was very good at her job, because she was so confident and caring towards her patients. I wanted to work in a specialized OB/GYN hospital (Zahash Gah, which was the same one we trained in) with some of my friends, but I didn't get in. So I took a job in the same hospital as Zaybah, in the Intensive Care Unit. I did not have any training for that, nor did they give me any. They hired me to work the night shift with two male nurses. I had no idea what I was doing, and the male nurses did most of the work. I was too passive to ask questions and learn, so I began to hate my job. I did not have any friends there either, because my friends from nursing school went to work for different hospitals.

I wanted to work with some of my friends in the military hospital, but I did not know how to go about it, so I asked my brother Amir. He went to the director of the hospital and inquired about getting me a job. The director used to teach at the nursing school I graduated from. She said, "Anisa was not one of my favorite people, because when I taught her, she appeared very stuck up and rude." She also said that she did not have anything against my brother, but she could not hire me for that reason. I, on the other hand, knew that I had never had her as a teacher. Probably because I was always shy and quiet, she must have assumed that I was not very friendly.

Amir was very upset with me for getting such a bad reputation. I told him, "I have no idea why she felt that way about me." I felt so defeated once again, but then I received a call from the new Auxiliary Nursing School director, Jamila-*jaan*. She wanted to interview me, and I was excited to meet her. She was a very good director, and worked at Zahish Gah nurse midwifery school before I attended that school to complete my nursing certification.

During the interview, she said, "I will only hire the best new graduates to teach in the new school that I'm starting." She was hiring nursing instructors for the new Auxiliary Nursing School, near the Wazir Akbar Khan Hospital in Kabul. It was a beautiful, modern school, built around 1975, and run by Americans. It was planned that a health care team, which included a doctor and two teachers, would go to villages in the provinces, talk to to schools, students and parents, and recruit girls into the nursing program. The students would be coming from villages across the country, after completing elementary or middle school. After studying for eighteen months, they would then go back to the villages and work in clinics, deliver babies, give shots, and help their communities. The school would provide room and board, and would not charge tuition.

Jamila said, "You could join us in this new project and teach when the time comes. You should have come to me when you graduated." I was so happy to hear that someone knew me and cared enough to find me and offer me a job. Jamila had just come back from her training in America. To me, she embodied the confidence, intelligence, and the modernity of America. I found myself drawn to her; she was such a good role model. She was everything I wanted to be.

Then she said, "One day, you might have the opportunity to go to America." For a few seconds, I had a vision of how my life would change if that really happened. I imagined how I could become like Jamila or have the confidence she exhibited. Deep down, I did not believe that could happen in a million years, but I said, "Yes, I'll accept the job."

How could I say "no" to such an influential woman? The position was so good and offered me so much potential. Jamila was happy that I accepted her offer, and she welcomed me to the new school and introduced me to everyone. I left and went home, then had a massive panic attack. I cried and cried, for my fears kept getting in the way of my happiness. How could I meet my potential when all of these fears took over my mind and body? Why is this happening to me? Why did God give me the talent but not the confidence to use it?

I could solve any algebra problem, or anything else for that matter, but could not figure out how to get rid of my fear. I came home and told my family about the offer. My mother was ecstatic about this, since it was a proper thing for a girl to be a teacher more than anything else. My oldest brother, Amir, was happy that I had found someone who believed in me and had offered me a job.

~ Eight ~

Becoming a Teacher

The school was almost ready to open. They were working on the furnishings and school curriculum. I was nervous at first, but found myself liking the idea of teaching girls ages 13-17 from different parts of the country. I teamed up with a senior instructor named Gole to teach obstetrics. Somehow, I had a different feeling when I spoke as a teacher, being an authority figure for the young students. I had much more confidence. Gole showed me how to have more confidence when I began to teach, just by watching her.

I took the students for their clinical rotations and really enjoyed teaching them everything I knew, and it made me realize that my knowledge was finally being put to good use. The students were young and enthusiastic. Some of them were shy, like me at their age, but I tried to get them out of their shells gently and slowly. These were girls who had been repressed. If it weren't for this school, they would have ended up getting married by the age of fifteen.

Some of girls' parents (especially their fathers), would not allow their daughters to go because they didn't want them to go to the city and learn new ideas. The health care team worked hard to convince them to allow the girls to leave their towns and attend the school.

There were no tuition or fees during the eighteen months of study, and that was a big incentive to let them attend school. These young girls became a huge asset to their community. Some liked the city lifestyle, and did not want to go back to work in rural areas. For those girls, they either took a job in the city or they went on to higher education. For me, it was a very rewarding job. The girls loved me as a teacher. In a real twist of fate, though, some of them thought that I was very strict. Perhaps that was a misconception everyone had about me. I did not express myself much, because I didn't feel comfortable.

My life suddenly changed when I became one of the candidates to join a group of six people to study English. If I studied hard and passed the TOEFL test, I could go to America in a year or two. Every morning we all went to class to study English, then in the afternoon we came to school to teach. I was getting anxious now due to the intense studying and hectic schedule.

I started to get panic attacks again when I went to classes. I tried to hide it, but sometimes I just could not. I was doing great with the tests, and I was actually helping some of my group members with English. I was proud of myself at times, but the fears kept coming back.

~~~

By now, all of my siblings were working and making money to pay for household items. *Mami* seemed very happy and our lives seemed to be getting better. She began to think about Amir and Zaman's future. They had just graduated from college. Amir majored in agriculture and Zaman in literature.

She wanted them to get married, so she began a search for the available pretty girls in the neighborhood. My mom was more open-minded than the rest of her family, so she checked with her sons first to make sure they liked the girls she picked out. She wanted them to get married at the same time because the groom's family is supposed to pay for everything, and that would be easier, financially. So, after much effort and persuasion of the girls' families, Mom found just the right girls for her sons to marry. They became engaged, and the wedding date was set for both couples to marry at the same time.

Amir's wife, Dela, is the sister-in-law of my cousin, and a few years younger than Amir. This is a good thing, because, in our culture a man does not want to marry an older girl – it is a sign of desperation. Zaman's future wife was in the same school as one of my half sisters, and she recommended her to mom. Zaman went to meet her first, and instantly liked her. Then my mom went to each of their houses and asked their parents for their daughters' hands a few times, until they agreed. Ria's parents wanted her to finish high school first, so Mom promised that Zaman would wait until she finished high school before they got married. And, that Ria would complete college after they get married. True to her word, Mom eventually kept her promise.

Now it was time for the engagement party. All of our relatives, friends and co-workers were invited to our home. We purchased all the food, arranged for the music and prepared the gifts. The party lasted all day with the meal preparation in my dad's first house by a male chef and the men of the family, and the tea, candy, cookies and cakes were also prepared there, too. The men gathered together in one house and the women gathered together in my Mom's house. There were six parties – each separated by men and women – because there would be some men that women are not related to. For very traditional women, the only men that they can show their faces to are husbands and blood relatives. Our family wouldn't have cared if men and women mixed together at a party, but we had to respect our relatives' wishes, as they were more conservative.

All my sisters, nieces and I welcomed the guests. Mom wanted to make sure everyone was seated, and served candy, pastries, and tea with cardamom as soon as they walked in the door. Zaybah and I were the hostesses, and between the engagement party and the wedding, we kept busy preparing special meals and taking food and gifts to the bride's house. This was during Eid, the holidays after the end of Ramadan, and Nowrose, the New Year.

There are two Eids every year. The first Eid is after Ramadan, the month when Muslims fast from sunrise to sunset. No food, drink or anything else is allowed to be taken by mouth. Afterwards, families celebrate by gathering, visiting their relatives, and eating. Two months later is the second Eid, Eid Qurban, which means "Feast of Sacrifice." This is when millions of Muslims go to Mecca. Everyone sacrifices sheep, cows or calves in the name of Alla. The meat is for themselves, but also given to neighbors, and to the poor.

Nowrose, or New Year, is the first day of the Pilgrim's calendar, which is observed in the Middle East. It happens on March 21st, the first day of spring. People celebrate the New Year by going to picnics, and preparing meals that consist of fried fish, *jelabie*, (a sweet pastry) white rice, spinach, and yogurt topped with brown sugar.

Before the wedding day arrived, we shopped for clothes, makeup, and jewelry for the brides and family members. All three houses hosted the wedding – Ria's, Dela's, and my mom's. Each family entertained their own relatives, and after entertaining all day, we decided to rent a private bus and celebrate at each family's home. We went to Ria's, and then Dela's, and the bride and groom came along in a car decorated with silk flowers. There were a lot of Volgas in Kabul at that time – fancy Russian cars. It was dawn when the wedding ceremony and celebration ended. We were so exhausted by the time we went home and finally got to sleep. Mom did not sleep much, because she had to take care of the overnight guests. In the morning, she prepared food and tea for them, but was very happy because her role as a mother was going well. There were still some complaints, disagreements, and some unhappy relatives and family members, but that is how it goes. Like they say, you cannot make everyone happy.

Both Amir and Zaman lived with their new wives in the same house we lived in, but in different sections. And everyone shared the yard. Mom still had Aman, Zaybah and me in the house. Zaybah and I didn't have much luck in getting married off, but it was better this way. Now, we were nineteen and twenty years old, and according to some of our relatives, we were already too old now. Once, Zaybah was going to be married off to one of my cousins. My uncle and aunt came to ask my parents for Zaybah's hand in marriage to their son. My parents agreed, but when my dad discussed the wedding arrangements with my uncle, her wedding expenses were too high for the groom's family. My uncle tried to bargain, but it did not work, as he was very cheap. I think that my dad did that on purpose, as he was not very fond of him. After that, my stepmom agreed to lower the expenses and offered her oldest daughter, Razy, to the cousin. This whole episode was a good thing for Zaybah, because Razy's life turned out to be like my youngest sister Rona's – she lived in the suburbs, sweeping floors, baking bread in the *tandoor*, washing clothes by hand and having a bunch of babies. Her in-laws constantly called her "the cheap wife," because they got such a good bargain.

My paternal grandmother came to visit us one day and saw me wearing a short-sleeved shirt and not wearing a headscarf. She suggested to me that I needed to cover my head and arms. Later on, she talked to my mom about needing to marry me immediately to one of the uneducated younger cousins.

"In addition," she said, "Anisa needs to stop going to school, quit her job and stay at home."

Mom said "no" to my grandmother. So my grandmother went over to Zewar's house to ask for her daughter to marry her grandson. My stepmother and my father said that they'd be willing to give up their daughter. As usual, my aunts and uncles asked *Mami* first, because they had to show her respect – she was the first wife. They came and asked her, even though they knew she would say "no" to their request. Zewar's second daughter, Asif, who was fourteen years old, became engaged to the uneducated suburban cousin. Her life turned out even worse than Razy's.

The next time someone wanted to get me married off, it was one of my students who wanted to match me with her oldest brother of seven kids. His mother came to our house, asking my mom for my hand in marriage to her son. I had never seen this man in my life, so that answer was, "no" again. My mother did not want Zaybah and me to have our lives ruined.

She encouraged us to be strong, independent women. We worked and took care of the house, but we did not let our *Mami* work at home much anymore. She had many health problems. Her body was prematurely aging, physically and emotionally. At fifty-five years old, she looked like a seventy-five-year-old woman. She had arthritis, gastritis, and reproductive problems, high blood pressure and many emotional problems. Her arms and legs hurt all the time, and she could not eat much of anything. Sometimes, her stomach would bloat and spasm so badly, that she could not catch her breath. Amir would have to massage her back and shoulders to get her to burp and relieve the bloating. Then she would be able to breathe again.

She kept saying that her uterus was hurting, and she thought she had a fibroid or a dead baby inside her womb. She told me that after my youngest sister Rona was born, she had all the signs of pregnancy for three months, and then all of a sudden it stopped. She said that she never got rid of that heavy, pregnant feeling. She felt ill every month, and we never had a doctor diagnose her condition.

My father always told her she was all right, and she kept talking to her nephew, Dr. Ghulam, who told her, "It is all in your head. You need to just relax and not worry." No one took her concerns seriously. To make things even worse, sometimes when she would get upset, she would start laughing uncontrollably for a few minutes, and then start crying. All of us would just look at her, not knowing what to do or say to stop her. So, Pari, Amir or Zaybah would just put their hands on her shoulders and let her rest on her side for a while. Mom would eventually just fall asleep. When she woke up, she could not remember anything that had happened.

I was very concerned for my dear mother, and was afraid that I would lose her. That is when I would have panic attacks, and pace the floors, holding the Quran to my chest, praying for my mother. After these episodes, I would lie down and almost pass out. My chest hurt, my whole body would be numb and sweaty – but I would think to myself, *I am all right. At least my mother is all right, and that's all that matters to me.*

Mom had beautiful long hair, and Zaybah or I would help her bathe, shampoo her hair, brush it out, and braid it. We bought her pain medicine, antacids, and the right foods and juices. We washed her clothes and ironed them. We made sure she had on the perfect outfit when she went to see her relatives. We took her in taxis instead of taking buses, so we could make things easier for her now that she was so fragile.

Mom suffered from loneliness, too, because her sons, Amir and Zaman, were busy with their own families and their work. Aman, Zaybah and I went to work. Zaybah worked at the hospital, mostly at night. Aman hung out with his friends and I was so preoccupied with my problems, that I was not good company for her. During this time, I missed Zaybah the most, and always felt better when Zaybah was home. Zaybah would sleep during the day, since she worked at night. Even when she did not work, she was always tired and slept all the time. I would try to wake her up when she did not work, but it usually just ended up making Zaybah angry, and she would start yelling at me for waking her up.

I used to go to the movies with my coworkers on Thursday afternoons. This did not make my mom very happy, because she wanted her twenty-year-old daughter to come straight home from work. Culture dictated that all the grown-up kids live together unless they are married – especially the girls. There was absolutely no dating or socializing with the opposite sex; it was not permitted in our culture.

~ Nine ~

Santa Cruz

In the fall of 1977, I took the TOEFL English exam and passed with the rest of my group. Now, it was time to get ready for the trip of a lifetime. I told my mother and brother about the possibility of going to America. My mom was not sure about letting her daughter go half way around the world to America. It was not like I had never travelled before, though. I had been on 1-2 week trips to the provinces of Afghanistan to recruit students for the school. But those trips were usually accompanied by a doctor, another nurse-midwife, and a driver. To my mother, this trip to America was too drastic. She was upset and kept saying, "no" to me leaving the country even for eight months. She told me that anything could happen. "You are a single girl," she said. "It will be a scandal if anything happened." She was worried about my honor. "In addition, all the relatives will criticize me for letting you go!" Also, she worried that I could become Western and forget about my culture and family.

Amir and the rest of the siblings were OK with it, but my father did not have much to say. He seemed quiet. I think he was secretly proud of me. My dad always wanted me to be a doctor, and I think he believed in me more than I did.

I eventually had to have one of my group members, a nursing teacher named Sohaila, come and talk to my mom and promise her that she would watch over me like a mother, since she had to leave her 3-year-old son and 6-year-old daughter behind with her husband. *Mami* hugged her and cried for the longest time.

The morning we were getting ready to go to the airport, mom had been crying all night. She did not want to go to the airport. I was actually scared to death just thinking about getting on my very first plane flight. The minute it took off, I started crying. I was sad, yet happy at the same time. I knew this was going to change my life forever. I saw my family wave goodbye from the upper level balcony of the Kabul airport.

It was harder for the group members who had to leave their children behind, especially for Sohaila. Sohaila's husband was in the military. He was very conservative, and she had never been on any trip before because of their young children. This was her first time. She had a teenage sister at home and brother that were taking care of her kids. At least I did not have to worry about all that. However, I was inexperienced and had never been on a plane before. I somehow still did not panic, though. I was looking forward to the trip as something that was taking me away from all the heartache of life in general in my home country.

We flew to London first, and then to Washington DC for a week of orientation. We studied in classrooms during the day, and had burgers and French fries at lunch. We ate more fast food for dinner, usually Kentucky Fried Chicken. The food was foreign to us, but oh, so good. We had a ball. We also marveled at the first time we went to an orchestral concert. It was outdoors with thousands of people. That night, we were having dinner at the biggest black-tie restaurant in the area. We all dressed up and had a fabulous dinner and dessert. We had to be careful not to go over the budget that was given to us, though, and were very aware of just how much everything cost.

We walked in the beautiful fall weather with yellow and red leaves falling all around. It was so beautiful that there were no words to describe it.

We were taken to one of the high schools in Washington, DC, where we sat in the back of the classroom. Watching the kids being so outgoing and free to talk amazed us. An African American male student happened to sit next to me, and jokingly asked me if I would marry him. I was about to die just hearing that proposal. I thought he was actually serious. I managed to move to another chair. My heart was racing. I was glad beyond belief when we left the school.

The day came when we left Washington, DC and headed to Santa Cruz, California. Each one of us was assigned to a host family. I went to this young couple's home, Susan and Steve. They were your "typical" American family with two kids. The 3-year-old boy was named Jay and the six year old was named Patrick. My classmates and I were separated from each other, except for every day in the classroom. That was definitely a challenging experience. We had to learn about the American lifestyle and get to know everyone in the family, including the grandparents. My host family was very interested in getting to know me. I went to their Thanksgiving and Christmas parties and met more people. I was amazed at how people were interested in how I lived, my family, and my background. I was the center of attention and I actually did OK.

Little Jay came every morning to my door, and called me "Alicia." He wanted to know if I was awake. I never knew why, but this seemed to make him happy. That meant that it was time to eat breakfast with them before I went to school. My host, Susan, made eggs and pancakes one day, and cereal and bananas the next. Apple juice was my favorite, and I had to drink a glass every day. Susan was in her late twenties or early thirties. She was tall and slim, had long, dark brown hair with some premature gray. She stayed home, took care of the kids and the house. Her husband, Steve, was a local pilot and engineer. He also owned a winery and was out of town a lot.

Susan spent a lot of time with the kids and now, me. At night, she helped me with the English lessons I took during the day. On one of those nights, Susan and 6-year-old Patrick were trying to explain the word "faces" to me, and how to pronounce the word. They were making all kinds of faces themselves, but it really seemed strange. Somehow, I was not convinced that was the correct explanation. Finally, I brought my notebook to show it to them. Susan and little Patrick were very embarrassed when they saw that the real word was "feces."

There were some other funny moments as well. One night, after spending time with the host family I excused myself, and told them I needed to go to the roof, meaning upstairs to my bedroom. That stirred up some laughter, but made me embarrassed, because I was not used to jokes – especially little kids laughing at an adult's mistakes.

Susan taught me how to ride my first bicycle down the hill near their home. There were a few times when I fell, and scraped my knees, shoulders and elbows. Once, when Susan was not home, Sohaila and I were riding the bicycle. I fell off the bike and hit my head (of course I had no helmet on), and the next day I could not get out of bed to go to school. I was dizzy and felt nauseated. The director of the program got upset with me for missing class. At the time, I don't think he realized how badly I was hurt. I probably had a concussion. Instead of having me checked by a doctor, the director told me that I could not miss school under any circumstances, and gave me my first warning. A sudden wave of homesickness overcame me, and I missed my mother like never before. I confided in Sohaila. She came after school, and tended to me, gave me cool washcloths, and fixed me some kind of soup. I couldn't get out of bed. Every time I tried, I got dizzy and threw up. Fortunately, the next day I felt better and made it to school. I never missed another day of school.

One night, Susan took her kids and me to dinner to an Italian restaurant. Susan's friend Kerry joined us. Kerry was very pregnant and divorced. When I heard that news, it made me very sad for her, since divorce was very uncommon in Afghanistan. I constantly told her how sorry I was for her situation, which made Kerry very uncomfortable. Kerry told me it was OK in this country to get a divorce. She told me actually, that was a good thing for her. That she was happy that she was divorced, and it was for the best.

Of course, I did not believe her. In my country, divorce rarely happened. I knew of one young woman in my uncle's neighborhood. Her very old husband had divorced her. He was like her grandfather, obviously it was an arranged marriage. She then married a younger man around her own age. No one would have anything to do with her anymore. Everyone talked very ill of her and her children. Men were the only ones that could divorce a woman. All they had to say was, "I divorce you, I divorce you, I divorce you," three times, in front of a Mullah or authority figure.

That night, I saw men and women walking around hand in hand, and kissing on the street. Music was playing outside the restaurant. People were dancing on the sidewalk. I just couldn't believe my eyes. What a country. It was amazing how people felt free and happy. Then we went to the beach. We stood on top of the rocks and watched the waves hitting the shore and washing the sand, and the little kids running around on the beach playing with sand and catching the waves. How beautiful it all was.

~~~

The training was part of a nurse practitioner and maternal and child health certification program. During the first two months, we attended intensive English classes. Two female instructors taught us from 8 am to 5 pm each day.

Sunday was the day we had off, and Saturdays were for field trips, like going to San Francisco, or whale watching. I remember going on a submarine under the sea, and looking at sea creatures. I wasn't used to being close to the water, so it was really scary when the ship took us down under the sea.

On the weekends, all of us Afghan girls would get together at one of our host's houses. We would dress up, take pictures, and have nothing but fun. Some weekends we would go shopping all day (if we could get a ride, since we did not drive). Those were the best of days.

The time went by quickly living with our host families. Almost without warning, it was time for two weeks of intensive training at a house on the beach, where we learned how to plan curricula and teach midwifery. There were bunk beds and a private chef who prepared three meals a day. We had two American male instructors and one female instructor. One of the male instructors was very handsome, and the other was a big guy who was very funny and gave us confidence. We could go anywhere with him. We had classes all day except for mealtimes. By the time evening came, we were so exhausted, we couldn't enjoy the rest of the day (or perhaps didn't know how to enjoy the time). It was springtime, and beautiful outside, but we were too shy and it wasn't our custom to go out to the beach and lie in the sun.

After that, they placed us in clinics although we still had classes during the morning hours. We rotated between Planned Parenthood, hospitals, home health care, and community hospitals. We visited a nursing school, observed birthing centers, placed IUDs, and watched abortions being performed. At the time, I just thought abortion was a common practice in America. I couldn't discern that only some people had abortions, and I didn't realize that there were people against abortion.

Sohaila constantly cried for her kids. Sheema and Mourie and I were the single girls who occupied ourselves with studying. Fatima was another single, older girl that enjoyed her independent life. She was a poet and struggled with the program due to her poor English. She was sensitive and traditional. Sohaila's cousin, Semon, was older and had kids back home, but you never saw her crying or being upset. She had been to Germany before, and was enjoying herself the most.

Two female students from Kenya were also in the group. They spoke perfect English. They were not a very friendly pair, though. They kept falling asleep in the classroom most of the time. It did not take much for them to learn things at all, which bothered us a bit. Unlike the six of us Afghan women (especially Fatima, Sohaila and Semon), they seemed almost too at ease with the program.

After the intensive program at the beach, we were finally given apartments – two women per apartment. I ended up being with Sohaila, Mourie with Sheema and Fatima with Semon (which turned out to be the worst match). Semon was very liberated and had a free spirit. She sometimes used beer or cooking wine in her dishes, whereas Fatima, a traditional Afghan woman, had very strict values. She brought some of her food to our apartment to cook, due to the fact that she did not want to use the same oven in which Semon poured wine on her food.

Once we started living in our own apartments, we felt freer. We could cook and do what we wanted to. We didn't have to worry about accidentally eating pork or shellfish or having alcohol in our drinks. I remember the day we went to a host's family friend house for a Saturday lunch. There was shrimp salad sitting on the table, and the host offered us to help ourselves. That did not go over well with Fatima, and she started crying, which made the hosts feel very bad. They weren't aware of the religious restriction. She said that the tiny little shrimp in the salad looked like worms to her.

I rode my bicycle to school back and forth. Some days I came home at lunch to check for mail from home, always looking for the mail carrier. We all were so homesick. Any kind of news from home was something we looked forward to. I went to the grocery store on my bicycle, and I was very proud of myself and of the independence that I was forging for myself.

Most of the time we all took two buses to and from school. Mourie was the only one who knew the bus schedule. She was the one we always asked for the bus time when we went anywhere.

I was almost hit by a van one time when I was riding my bike, since I did not know I was supposed to stop at the stop sign. That incident left my heart pounding. The driver sped up to avoid hitting me, and my bike hit the back of his van. The driver stopped to see if I was OK. He was nice, but was not very happy. He yelled at me, "Don't you know how to stop at the stop sign?" I was too shy to say, "No, I do not know, I just started learning how to ride my bike. No one explained the traffic rules to me!" All I could say was, "I am sorry," and try to hide my panic. I learned my lesson after that incident.

One time Sohaila and I invited our hosts to dinner at our apartment with the rest of the girls. All of the Afghan girls wanted to show their hosts their appreciation for the time we spent in their homes. Dinner was excellent, and everyone enjoyed themselves. We usually washed dishes by hand, but tonight was different. We were going to show off our dishwasher. We loaded the dishwasher for the first time and within a few minutes the soapsuds from the dishwasher were covering the entire kitchen floor. We were all screaming and laughing in the kitchen, and our visitors were wondering what had happened. We found out that one of us had used regular hand washing dish detergent. It took every one in the apartment to clean up the mess. Our hosts gave us the name of a special detergent we were supposed to use, called Cascade. We wrote it down so we wouldn't forget the name. I do not think we were ever so embarrassed before.

We had a spending allowance for our daily meals and transportation, and we were very frugal. Usually, between Sohaila and me, we each spent about $20.00 a week for our groceries (this was good old 1978). We never ate out, and we were able to save a little money. When it was close to the time to go back home, we spent most of our time shopping for little gifts for our family, like shampoo, lipstick and perfumes. We constantly weighed our suitcases to make sure that they weren't over the limit. Even though we loved Santa Cruz and the freedom we had become used to, we were so excited about going back home. We were ready to go back. I missed my mom more than I could admit even to myself.

The morning of my flight to America. From left to right: me, my mother, and my youngest brother, Aman. I was 19.

~ Ten ~

Coming Home to Chaos

We were all set to return home, only to find that things were changing very quickly. Unfortunately, 1978 was also the year that President Mohammad Daoud was assassinated. The government was overthrown, and the Communist Party took control. From peace, all hell suddenly broke loose. The news was big on this subject, talking about the destruction, and the number of people who were dead, and all the commotion that was going on. We couldn't get letters from our families anymore, which was the most distressing part of all. We became really anxious and worried.

We were ready to go home and see it for ourselves. We wanted to make sure our family members were alive and well, and as soon as we finished the program we went back home without delay.

Once we returned to Afghanistan, things didn't seem as bad as we had heard. The media had made it seem worse than it was. There wasn't as much violence on the street and things seemed calm. We were happy to see our families and everything appeared to be OK. Until we went back to work, that is. The biggest change was that we had a new communist regime now. We were all immediately pressured into joining the Communist Party, and cheering the new regime and the new revolution publicly, on the streets.

The new director of the nursing school was also head of the Communist Party women's group. Sohaila and I couldn't speak openly about anything, because we had just come from the USA. We were more of a target of suspicion based on how we reacted to the new regime, and we were put under more pressure than the others to take steps to promote communism. Sohaila was the assistant principal, and since I was her best friend, I wanted to support her. We wore military uniforms and marched on the streets of Kabul. That didn't go over well with the rest of the group. They didn't participate much and tried not to get involved except for Semon, who was the director of the Children's Hospital. She only marched because she wanted to save her job.

Life was getting harder. We had to watch what we discussed as far as politics went. Schoolchildren were actually encouraged to be spies in their own homes. The teachers were forced to ask children at school, "What did you talk about at home last night? Who did you spend time with?" The children were brainwashed to report anything their parents were discussing against the communist regime. The teachers convinced the children to do this because, "This regime is going to save our country, and you have a duty to help," they said.

The government would then go to the kids' homes and arrest the parents based on what these little kids reported. Most of those parents were jailed, put to death or just "disappeared," and never came back home. There were days that bombs were going off in the middle of the afternoon, while we were on our way home, and it seemed as if "someone" – an opposition group – was trying to fight back. As a result, the government would go to people's homes at night for any suspicious reason that they could think of, and arrest the head of the family, and place him in Pul-e-Charkhi. Pul-e-Charkhi was the biggest and most notorious prison in Kabul, and it was filling up quickly. They had to make room for more, so the Soviet-backed Communist Party and the military would line up people in the middle of the night and shoot them. They bulldozed the ground and buried them half-dead.

People said the ground shook after the prisoners were buried alive. Some managed to dig their way out, and these stories were told by those who survived. In addition to everything that they had been through, they had somehow escaped the grounds of the biggest prison in the history of Afghanistan.

My uncle Khan, my mom's youngest brother, was a military general at the time, and was also actually in Pul-e-Charkhi for a while. He witnessed these sights every single night in prison. And every night he was fearful, because when the guards came and called out people's names, they took them, and those people never returned.

A new group was born as a result of these atrocities. This collection was the Mujahidin (freedom fighters). They also went to people's homes, workplaces, or to the streets, taking young boys and training them to become fighters against the government and the communists. The Mujahidin also forcibly took some of the military leaders to lead their groups. If they didn't agree to join, they made sure they didn't return home alive.

Again, my poor uncle Khan got the short end of the stick. Because he was a general, as soon as he was released from prison, the Mujahidin took him and another young military leader up to the mountains into a cave near his home. They tied them up and tried to persuade them to lead their group. When the young military leader didn't agree, they took him out of the cave, and my uncle never saw him again. But my uncle proved that he was a survivor and that he was smarter than others. He readily agreed with them to cooperate, just to buy himself time to escape, which is exactly what he did.

The Mujahidin came back to his home to search for him again. His wife and thirteen children were devastated. His wife told the Mujahidin that he never returned and let them search the house. They determined that he somehow died, and left his home and didn't bother them again. In reality, Khan had escaped through the mountains, into the dry, dusty 110-degree heat of summer, and crawled down the slopes. He was fatigued and dehydrated. He had to drink his own urine, as unpleasant as it sounds, in order to survive. He hid during the day and walked at night.

He made it alive to our house after a few days, and he didn't let anyone know he was there except for my mom. She had prayed every second of every day for her brother to come home, and was so relieved when he did.

When his family learned that he was alive, it was the happiest day for them. His wife knew his heart, and knew that he was strong-willed. Deep down, she knew he was alive. Since the Mujahidin had lost him, it meant that he had escaped somewhere. He was like my grandmother; he could survive starvation and dehydration or anything fate could throw at him. He was a military man, and didn't believe in being weak. He had thirteen children and just had to come back to them. That was his mission – to come back and be with his family. And that is what he did.

He told me that story a couple years ago, and as he was telling me, the hair on my skin was standing up.

I asked him, "How did you do it?"

"God gave me the strength and patience. And if you are a true believer in God, and have a strong faith, you can make it through anything," he said. That is my uncle Khan. Just like my mom, strong-willed and courageous.

~~~

As the fighting continued between the Russian military and the Mujahidin, I slept only every other night. I was constantly scared that they were going to come in to our home, take my brothers and rape us, which was usually what happened to other families. The gunfire and bombs made me pace the house all night. I was always glad when morning came. Then I did not have to worry so much.

One afternoon, when I was in the school van coming home from work, the bombs started going off and gunshots rang out. The driver of the van became very concerned and told me to get down. I had to duck my head down in back seat of the van. Gunshots were actually hitting the van. I was glad when I got home. I asked the driver to come into our home so he could be safe, too.

An hour later, bombs started going off again from Balahisar, the military base which was close to our home. It felt like they were falling right on top of our house. Our whole family was screaming and running around the first floor, trying to avoid the bombs. Amir, my oldest brother, was upset with everyone for being out of control. He tried to calm us down.

"Don't scream," he said. "If it is meant for a bomb to hit us, it will regardless, so don't be so weak." That did not help me – it only made matters worse. I was in a panic and didn't know what else to do.

Bombs hit some of the homes nearby. People were running for their lives – away from the city to the suburbs – in order to escape the bombs. We were no different from anyone else, and found ourselves running too. Women in *chaderi*s, little children, everyone was running. After a few miles, we got to the suburbs and couldn't run anymore. So we walked. Eventually, my whole family ended up in Benehisar at my uncle Aji's home, ten miles away from the city. We spent the night there, but we could not sleep the whole night.

The next day when we returned, we couldn't believe our house was still standing. The work van had a few more bullet holes from gunshots, though. The driver had stayed at our house that night as well, finally returning to his home the next day.

There was a 10 pm curfew, so wherever we were, we made sure to get home before 10 pm. If you dared to do otherwise, you were approached by Afghan or Russian military men with guns and searched. If you were suspected of opposing the Communist Party, you could be taken in and interrogated. Mom now feared the loss of her sons. If they came home later than 6 or 7 pm, she would start crying and praying, and waiting for them by the door. All mothers feared losing their sons and husbands, and worried that their daughters would be kidnapped and raped.

People tried to leave the country. They made plans to escape the violence and go to refugee camps in Pakistan, Iran, or other countries. After a long red tape process, it was possible to obtain refugee status in those countries, but only if you had money. A lot of people were turned back. Our family also discussed this at times, but my brothers couldn't come to an agreement. Aman, my youngest brother, kept promising to get a bus and take the whole family over the border to Pakistan or Iran. However, he was unable to follow through.

My aunt Sofia's husband was in Germany. He made the decision for their family to go to Pakistan and try to get to Germany from there. That gave Zaman, my middle brother, the idea to leave with them to Pakistan. He started making plans.

Zaman and his wife Ria had a 3-year-old daughter and a 2-month-old son at the time. I had delivered my nephew at home, just as Ria and I had planned.

I was a new nurse/teacher, and found that in my job I was getting braver. Everything was going really well on the job. One day, I came home from work at 2 pm to find that Ria was in active labor. Both her mom and my mom were waiting for me. We both took a nap, and when Ria woke up, she wanted to push. In a matter of minutes, she had the most beautiful and healthy little boy, delivered by me. I was so proud of myself, and of the beautiful little nephew I brought into this world. They named him Aisal. He had light skin and chubby cheeks.

A few months later, my sister Rona was also ready to deliver. It was going to be with my help or that of an older dia (dias were experienced, older village midwives with no education who helped deliver babies at home). At that time, I never felt OK with those doulas delivering babies. There was a high mortality rate from these home deliveries, and I didn't want Rona to suffer. I had gained a lot of experience, so, I delivered my sister's baby at home. She bled a little, but everything was OK, and I had another beautiful nephew, named Farhad.

One day, Sohaila and I came home from work, and Amir's wife, Dela, was in active labor. She could not make it to the hospital. Both of us delivered her baby, and she also had a beautiful, healthy little boy. They named him Sameer. With God's help, all these deliveries went great.

Zewar, my stepmother, had always had good and fast deliveries. She was ready to have her eighth child. My father had confidence in me and asked me to deliver her baby. None of my sisters, my stepmother, Zewar, or my mom ever had any prenatal care. Zewar

went into labor in the middle of the night, and I was supposed to
be her nurse. My dad made it clear that he was available if I needed
him. I sat by her side all night and tried to deliver the baby. I was
monitoring her contractions with my hands like in the hospital, but
I had no way to listen to the baby's heartbeat. In those days, that is
how it was in Afghanistan, even in the hospitals. In the dawn hours,
she delivered a baby girl. It was stillborn.

Her face was disfigured and malformed; she had no eyes, nose
or mouth. Her face was all just flat tissue, but from the neck down
everything else was normal. She had a beautiful body with no face.
Zewar started to bleed profusely after she delivered the baby. I had
Zaman get a cab and took her to the hospital, where she was treated
and kept overnight. At least her life was saved.

At first, my stepmom blamed my father for the stillborn baby.
My father had been withdrawing fluid from her navel throughout
her pregnancy. Zewar had probably had a small hernia, and every
time it swelled like a small balloon, father relieved it with a syringe.
Later on, whenever she would fight with us, she blamed me for
killing her baby. That was the most traumatic experience I ever
had. I had nightmares for a long time. How could my dad put me
through that kind of experience? He delivered all of her babies
before this, why not this one? What was he thinking? Did I know
more than he did? No, I was a new graduate with no experience or
equipment.

I promised myself I would never deliver another baby at home
after that. Then one day, my aunt came home with her unmarried
daughter, who was complaining of abdominal pain.

My aunt said, "Can you take care of her?"

They didn't mention she was pregnant. I looked at my cousin
and said, "Oh my God, you are pregnant and in active labor." I was

not going to take another chance of delivering this baby at home. Therefore, I took my cousin outside the house and was waiting for a cab to take her to the hospital.

My cousin couldn't wait for the cab, she kept saying, "It's coming, it's coming." Therefore, I had to take her back home, and delivered a healthy baby girl. It was an uneventful birth. I was very grateful to God for helping me in this situation.

Immediately, before the baby began to cry, my cousin's mother wrapped the baby in a blanket and took it to the mosque. She didn't want anyone to hear it cry. She gave it to the Mullah and said, "You need to give this baby to somebody, somebody who wants a child." It would have been shameful to keep the child, because everyone would have known it was born out of wedlock. In fact, if my cousin's father or brothers had found out that their unmarried sister or daughter had a child, they may have killed her.

Only a few years ago, when I went back to Afghanistan, I learned what happened to that baby. The Mullah and his wife raised the baby girl themselves, in the mosque.

If it has not become clear yet, I am a big believer in God. I often turn to God to give me strength and help me do what I need to do.

~ Eleven ~

The Journey Begins

In September 1980, my brother Zaman finally decided it was time to leave the country. I had actually saved about $150 from my time in America – and it came in handy when I asked Zaman to take me along. Zaman agreed. My sister Zaybah wanted to go too. Unfortunately, she did not have that kind of money. For us, $150.00 was a little over 5,000.00 Afghani, almost three months' salary for a nurse in Kabul at that time.

We were waiting for the right opportunity to leave with the *khachak bar* – the man we were paying to smuggle us over the border. We paid him 5,000.00 Afghani for each person. In the meantime, mom was very distraught at the thought of having two of her kids leave the country any day now. She cried day and night, but she knew this was the right thing to do. The smuggler was arranged by an acquaintance named Mohammed. He lived in Jalalabad, approximately 100 miles east of Kabul.

Zaman was working for The British Council, as a conference manager, and was in danger due to his job. And I had been trained in the USA. We were constantly targeted and questioned, and they had already detained Zaman once before. Both of us felt like we were being watched, and we needed to leave. There was no help from any of the foreign agencies - they were in fear for their own lives.

My aunt Sofia, Ria and I were ready with our *chaderi*s and traditional clothes – clothes we did not normally wear. My best friend, Sohaila, knew about our plan and was going to miss me. But we didn't dare tell anyone else. She visited me often at this point. She comforted my mom and assured her that I would be OK.

Then the day came. I was in school, and I had just started my day at 8:30 in the morning. I got a call from my brother Zaman that I needed to make some kind of excuse and come home. I started panicking. I told the school principal that my nephew had fallen out of the window and I needed to take him to the hospital. But I whispered to some of my friends as I was hugging them, "It's time to leave." I said goodbye to them, and tears were running down my cheeks. Sohaila joined me, and we went home.

As soon as I got home, my aunt Sofia, her daughter and her two sons, my middle brother Zaman, his wife Ria, and their kids, and even Zaybah were ready. All nine of us were ready to make our escape. We had no idea how we would go, the route or the plan – all we knew was that we were leaving Kabul to go to Jalalabad, to my aunt's house.

Zaman was going to help Zaybah with money, so she decided to go too, which made me very happy. We all put on our *chaderi*s and took a small bag of clothes with us. Zaybah and I wore our mom's dresses and long white pants under her old grey and blue *chaderi*s. Everything was dark-colored except for our white pants and our sandals, and it was about 100 degrees out and dusty.

We all went to say goodbye to my father and to get his blessing. He told us he didn't have any problems with us leaving. He wished us luck and hugged us. We all kissed his hands, and he kissed our foreheads. Tears were rolling down his cheeks and ours, too.

I will never forget that day. I could tell that my dad was saying his last goodbye to us. We didn't know if we would ever be able to return or see him again. Mom said goodbye to us in the passageway outside the door. She hugged Zaman for the longest time, sobbing. She hugged me as long as she could, and told us, "These are my last goodbyes until I see you in heaven." She hugged Ria and her precious grandchildren, 3-year old Lela and 2-month old Aisal, for the last time.

When she turned to Zaybah, she could not say goodbye anymore. She asked Zaybah with her pleading eyes, "Are you leaving me too?" As a result, Zaybah changed her mind at the last second.

"No, Mom. I am not going to leave you. I am staying right here with you. I am never going to leave you." She turned to Zaman and me and she said, "I am sorry, I can't leave mom." I was upset but happy that she stayed with mom. I knew my mom had to have someone with her, or she probably wouldn't have made it through that very day.

Then we were all rushed out of the house and into a cab, sitting on top of each other in all the heat and in all those clothes. We headed towards Jalalabad. Even though we were hidden beneath our *chaderis*, we were scared to death, thinking, what if we are caught? We felt like the fugitives that we were. We felt like the whole world knew we were escaping.

We knew we were never going to come back. We were saying our goodbyes to the place we were born and raised, and we could not help sobbing for leaving our land – this precious country, which at one time was our heaven, and we were once so proud of.

As we were escaping, I felt that we were betraying our country, our family and our people. I felt guilty for leaving my mother. I felt like maybe I didn't love my mother as much as my sister Zaybah did. I felt like I was the inconsiderate, cold, unaffectionate daughter.

The cab passed through the city of Kabul, and we were on our way to the suburbs. The weather was hot, as it was in the middle of July. We were sweating under the *chaderis* and the road was dusty. I was getting claustrophobic under the *chaderi*, but afraid to lift up the veil that covered my face. All I could see through was the rectangular net over covering my eyes. The cab was packed with all of us – my aunt and her three kids, my brother Zaman, his wife Ria, my little niece and nephew and me. We stopped in a crowded *Chai Khana* (café) to eat lunch, but we did not have much appetite at all.

We finally got to Jalalabad in the afternoon. We arrived at my aunt Sofia's winter home, part of which was rented out to people my aunt knew. We all slept in one big room, on the floor, for the following week. At night, we would constantly wet our feet with cold water to cool off. The weather was hot and humid, with only a single fan to cool us off.

Even here, we could hear gunshots and bombs going off repeatedly. The tenants were talking about people following us and knowing about our escape. They scared us to death.

The smuggler came and told us that the money we gave him wasn't enough. We needed to get some more money in order to get out of the country. Zaman had to go back to Kabul and borrow money from my youngest brother, Aman. When Mom saw Zaman coming back, she got very excited, thinking we were all coming back. That was not true, and when Zaman told her the real reason, she went through the same trauma again. Aman, my youngest brother, helped Zaman and lent him some money.

On his way back to us, Zaman was stopped by the military and questioned about where he was going. It took some persuasion for Zaman to be released. He was very happy when he joined his wife, kids, and everyone else back in Jalalabad. It was as if a small victory had been won in a long war.

We were waiting for the right time to go through the border, and everyone was on edge. One late evening, the smuggler came and told my aunt Sofia, Zaman and me to get ready to leave. The utility truck was waiting for us. We were going to go to the city of Kameh, to the next smuggler's house, and the truck driver knew exactly where to go. The plan was that Mohammed was going to bring Ria and her children and Sofia's kids in another car. In order to get through the border, he would provide a doctor's letter stating that Ria, her children, and my cousins were going to Pakistan for medical treatment.

My brother Zaman, my aunt Sofia and I said our goodbyes to my cousins, niece, nephew and sister-in-law, and got into the big, old semi-truck that was provided by our escape guide. Zaman sat next to the driver, and I sat between him and Sofia. The truck driver was driving on the uneven dirt road, and the evening was getting darker. The dust blowing in through the broken windows of the truck was unbearable, and even though the thick, hot *chaderi*s covered us completely, dust was sticking to our bodies and faces.

I remember there was a full moon. Stray dogs were barking in the distance. There was no one else on the long, winding, dirt road. None of us made a sound.

After a few miles, the truck driver stopped suddenly when two military men approached the truck with their machine guns. They looked inside to see us two women wearing *chaderi*s and the semi-local man accompanying us. Zaman was wearing the traditional Afghan man's long shirt with long baggy pants. He was unshaven and wearing an embroidered cap on his head. They ordered Zaman and the truck driver to get out of the truck. Zaman was scared but composed. They took them to the back of the truck for questioning. We couldn't see or hear anything from where we were sitting, but it seemed like eternity by the time Zaman returned.

In the meantime, I was shaking, holding the Holy Quran that my mom had given me pressed to my chest praying, "Oh *Khodaa-jaan* (God) please help us."

Sofia kept telling me, "Be brave and don't say anything. And stop shaking." But ironically, Sofia was shaking and holding her Quran to her chest, too.

"Let me see your military ID card," one of the guards said to Zaman. "Where are you taking these women?"

"I'm taking my mother and sister to a relative's house in Pakistan for medical treatment, and then I will return." They were satisfied with that answer and let him go. Zaman was so relieved. He returned to the truck at last, and the military guards with guns gave the driver permission to go. Zaman told us the men spoke *Pashto*, the common countryside language. Fortunately, he knew how to speak *Pashto*. The guards actually told the driver not to stop again for anyone else.

We arrived at the village where a second guide lived with his brothers and their families. He was supposed to take us on the second part of our journey, over the Torkham Pass to Pakistan. We arrived at a big compound, where about 20-30 people lived, surrounded by high walls and a small gate. The women of the family welcomed Sofia and me onto a mud porch, while Zaman stayed with the men of the village. Some of the men carried machine guns. Even though Zaman wanted to stay with us, men and women had to be separated in this traditional village. We were served dinner consisting of soup with bread, for which we had no appetite.

At some point during the night, there were gunshots and bombs going off. All of us had to run into the dark, windowless mudroom to hide. After a few minutes, when our eyes got used to the dark, we noticed that it was full of women and children. They were staring at us strangers, as their eyes were more focused in the dark. It was also full of baby goats, sheep and calves. There were about twenty-five people and fifteen animals in all. The smell in the room was unbearable. We were glad when they told us that we could go back to the porch.

Later that night, our escape guide's brothers were arguing over the money. Sofia and I could hear them right outside the gate. We couldn't understand them, but we could hear the loud disagreement and became quite concerned. Zaman got worried, as he couldn't trust these men. They were insisting on more money to take us over the pass.

It was very late when everyone quieted down and went to sleep. All of them were sleeping in the same room – men, women and baby goats and sheep. Since we were the guests, Zaman, Sofia and I each slept on a wooden, ropey bed on the porch. There were cows and donkeys ten feet away from us in the yard, and it got a little noisy in the middle of the night.

I was lying on the bed, looking at the full moon and stars with my heart pounding hard. I couldn't help thinking bad thoughts. *What if the gunmen burst in through the gate and start shooting? What if the gunmen are right inside these high walls and inside the big mudroom? What if we are raped and killed by these men, just because we are different from their wives?* I could not sleep at all that night. I noticed Zaman and Sofia were also tossing and turning – they couldn't sleep either.

As the stars and the moon slowly disappeared and daylight emerged, we were still unsure what was going to happen next. Zaman was trying to find out, because as far as we knew, there was no plan for us to be taken across the Torkham Pass by these men.

The next day, the men were gone all day, and the women were in the outdoor kitchen cooking and cleaning and preparing lunch and dinner. They were baking bread in the clay oven, boiling water and cooking on an open fire. We were just sitting on the porch in the hot sun, looking at these women, and thinking that our lives weren't so bad, compared to these women. Although at that moment, I was not quite so sure. I asked myself, *why are we taking such a risk? Why come all this way to be in more danger?* At that point I wanted to be home. I missed my mom already.

~~~

As it got dark, we were not looking forward to another dreadful night. Suddenly, without warning, we got the news at around 7 pm from the smuggler – "Get ready to leave." We were excited and scared at the same time; but at least we didn't have to spend another night in terror in that place. There was only one guide this time, a with a skinny little donkey. He was going to take us across the mountains on foot. He told us, "It's going to be a short distance, about two hours at most." Our belongings – just two bags – were loaded on the poor donkey.

We walked as fast as we could for the first two hours, without any problems. We still were dressed in our *chaderi*s and sandals. After two hours of brisk walking, we could not see any signs of life except for more mountains. The guide told us, "another half hour," and then another and another – he just kept lying.

At midnight, we joined a caravan of about 100-150 people, all of them going through the same journey. Except they were better equipped than we were. We didn't even have water with us. These people were more familiar with the area and were more experienced, and their smugglers did not cheat them as much. Ours didn't tell us anything – how far it was, or that we should bring water or food. Seeing more people and families made us feel better.

At one point during our walk, the guide yelled at everyone in the caravan, "Drop to the ground and don't move! There's a group of burglars or militia coming!" All 150 of us dropped to the ground, face down. While lying on the ground, I was praying hard to God again. I was scared to death throughout the whole journey, but nothing scared me more than this. I had heard about these crimes. The looters knew we had all of our money and valuables with us, and I truly thought that I was about to be raped and to be killed.

After 5-10 minutes, they told us, "You are safe. Keep on walking - the danger has passed." We were dragging by now. We had been walking about ten hours with no water and no proper shoes. Our *chaderi*s were getting heavier and hotter, and we could barely see where we were going. Our sandals were falling apart, and our feet and toes were bleeding now.

By sunrise, we arrived at a dirty pond, where everyone sat down by the water – including the donkeys, mules and horses. People were washing their faces and drinking water from the pond. After we had been drinking as much as we could, we finally smelled the strong odor of the water, where the animals had been drinking and peeing as well.

From this point, we still had to walk another couple of hours.

However, we never got the correct distance from the guide. He always said, "Another half an hour." I could not walk any more. Zaman was forced to drag me, with my arm around his shoulders. I felt bad for him, as he was as tired as I was, but he felt responsible for his sister. Sofia had to ride on the poor, exhausted donkey with the two bags already on him. We took breaks now and then, but we still had to get to where the second part of the journey would begin.

~ Twelve ~

Crossing the Torkham Pass

We stopped in the first village we arrived at, and had hot tea and bread in a little *Chai Khana*. The tea and bread tasted so good, and we regained some energy. We washed our faces and drank water that was cleaner than the pond water we drank before. It felt so good to be able to take a little break and drink.

The second part of the journey over the mountains had started. We still didn't know what was going to happen next. Fortunately, on the first day of the second leg, we had transportation, although it took some persuasion for me to get on it. Mules were provided for us, and I had never ridden a horse, mule or anything else in that category. I was dumbfounded as to how they worked.

"This is the only way to make it through the mountains," they told us.

I said, "It's OK, I'll walk!"

They helped me get on the mule, saying, "No, you're not."

I was scared and screaming. Sofia was better at it than I was. Zaman's mule was in front of us, and we were surrounded by the rest of the 100 or more people. There was no actual road, but just a narrow pathway for the mule's footsteps. With a canyon on one side and a high mountain cliff on the other, the mules were trained for these trips and were very careful. Even so, I was holding my breath for any sudden movements the mule made.

There were some funny moments. We laughed when the mule my aunt Sofia was riding sniffed my mule's butt. Then Zaman's mule went crazy at one point. He got too close to the big rocks on the mountain. Zaman's arm brushed against the rock, he got a big cut on his forearm, and it started gushing blood. Of course, being the nurse that I am, I tore the side of my *chaderi* to use it as a bandage to stop the bleeding, and we just continued on our trip as if nothing happened.

We started around 7 am, and rode the mules until 7 pm. We arrived at another little village. The guide told Zaman, "We have to spend the night here." He took a look around, and could only see Pashtun men with guns on their shoulders. It made Zaman uncomfortable, and he told the guide, "That is not possible. We have to keep going." It was getting dark. The smuggler agreed to take us to a bus station. We got on the bus with some other people. Suddenly the bus driver said, "I'm not going to drive unless people pay me more." The bus was full of tired families with little children. We had to pay him extra to take us to the border of Pakistan. We were happy that at least we did not have to walk or ride the mules anymore.

It took about two hours to get to the Torkham border, where a lot of people were being smuggled across to Peshawar, Pakistan. The border was crowded with many Pashtun men wearing traditional long shirts with matching baggy pants and black turbans, holding rifles. They spoke *Pashto* only. The hotel we spent the night at was another big, mud warehouse with those handmade ropey beds, and filled with refugees like us, but with only women and children inside. The men were camping outside, to guard their families.

Sofia and I were again given one bed for the two of us. We shared it, curled up head to toe. Zaman bought us Pakistani tea, made of more milk than tea. Sofia instantaneously fell asleep with her *chaderi* on. I managed to get a couple sips of the tea. It tasted like heaven to me, especially after the long trip, and walking and riding the mules for two days. We were extremely dehydrated. Then, I also fell fast asleep, still wearing my *chaderi*.

Zaman, on the other hand, never slept. He guarded us, because there were men coming and going constantly, to get supplies from the back of the warehouse. The next day, Zaman told Sofia and me that there were huge rats in the warehouse too. Luckily we didn't know. Even if we did, in reality it probably would not have mattered. We were just that exhausted.

The next morning we got back on the bus. We were so happy we did not have to walk again, but our hips and bottoms were hurting from the day before. The bus took us from the Torkham border to Peshawar. We got to Peshawar in the early afternoon, and went to Sofia's relatives' house.

For the next week, Sofia and I slept. We woke up only when the family was serving our meals or massaging our blistered, sore feet and backs.

Zaman, on the other hand, spent the next week at the bus station, waiting for his wife and children and Sofia's kids. He wore his traditional, long, gray shirt with matching baggy pants. He did not even want to shave anymore. Every evening, he seemed very tired and frustrated when he returned without his family. There was no way of communicating with Mohammad or with Zaman's wife.

After a week of constant waiting, they finally arrived. Both families were at last reunited with their kids, and everyone was very excited that we had made it through the worst part of the journey.

Sofia and Ria both lost their jewelry and some expensive items in the process. Mohammad had my aunt's and Ria's jewelry, including their wedding rings. He told them, "Give me all your jewelry, it's not safe to take it over the border, and I will bring it to you later." But of course he never did. They were very upset and never forgot that. In the end, though, none of that mattered, since we had made it safely to this point, to Peshawar.

My aunt's in-laws gave us a little guest room, and we spent the next two months there, all nine of us. We slept on the floor. On one side Sofia slept with her kids, and on the other side Zaman with his wife and kids. I slept by the door on top of the smelly, dusty shoes. We waited every single day to find a way to get out of Pakistan. There were more people and moneymaking crooks always making promises, but no action. Sofia's husband knew that we were in Pakistan, and he was trying to find a way to make arrangements for his wife and children to come to Germany.

Zaman had to do his own homework – he didn't have anyone helping him figure out how to get us out of Pakistan. Pakistan's embassy was no help; there were already tons of immigrants and refugees there. There were traffickers at bus stations and in the neighborhood that offered to send us somewhere for money, but many of them were liars. Zaman had to be careful, and he got very disappointed at times. At one point, he even told his wife Ria and me, "Go back home while I try to find a way." Ria and I were not going to through that again; but we were afraid it might happen. We were very frugal with the money we had.

We cooked very simple meals at home for both families and had been eating only rice and beans until now. Most of the meat was not clean. But one night we slaughtered and cooked a whole chicken that turned out to be very interesting. Lela (my niece) pulled the chicken platter close to her and she would not let anyone touch it. She kept saying, "I'm going to eat the whole thing." It took awhile to convince her that it was for everyone.

We were glad on the days we could have milk instead of tea for breakfast. Sofia's boys, Wes and Eas were ready to run and buy it from neighbors. We didn't trust the milk from stores, which were so dirty and dusty, with flies everywhere. We cooked potato skins, potatoes, rice and beans. And on good nights, usually we ate soups and more soups.

We all got along really well. We had a lot of fun, and laughed at the way we were living now. We had running water outside the door by way of a little stream. We washed our clothes and dishes there. We brushed our teeth from it too, until the day we watched a woman washing her baby's dirty diaper in the same stream. After that, we decided that it would be best to go to the other side of the village to fetch clean water for everything.

Sofia and Zaman were in charge of finances, and they were holding on to our money tightly. It was easy to see why they were being so frugal, because we did not know what was going to happen next or how long we would be staying in that little hole.

At night, we went to the bathroom outside in the open field – we didn't even have an outhouse. There was only one outhouse for the whole compound, and we didn't like to use it at night, when all the men would come home. We didn't want to chance crossing paths with any men using the same bathroom. Some days we went out with Sofia's relatives to the shopping center, and watched while they purchased stuff and ate lamb kabobs and fried fish. We also visited some other Afghans who lived nearby, the people we fetched water from. They were pretty well off; the husband was a businessman, and had a big home with running water.

Zaman and Sofia went to the embassy in Islamabad to try to obtain visas for us many times without any success. Finally, Zaman paid someone to get us round-trip tickets to Istanbul, Turkey. We needed to look as if we were coming back to Pakistan. He spent most of the money we had. He told us, "We have to make a leap of faith, as this is the only way we can get out of Pakistan."

After two months, we could finally get rid of our baggy, pastel colored Pakistani Panjabi (or *kurta*, a long shirt with baggy pants) and *Mami-jaan's* old *chaderi*s. We knew we were not going to need those anymore. After all, we were going to the modern country of Turkey. We wore our jeans and regular shirts. We still wore our scarves – we could not go without them just yet.

Both 3-year-old Lela and 4-months-old Aisal were dressed up for the occasion. Lela was in colorful Punjabi clothes, and Aisal was in a cute baby outfit. We were taken by cab to a fancy hotel in Islamabad. The door attendant opened the door for us. We saw the rooms with the beautiful decor and queen size beds, and felt like we were reborn from all those days stuck in the little guest room. We were there for only three or four hours, but we made the most of every single second. We took hot showers, since we had bathed with only a bucket of water that day, as usual. It felt good.

We ate the best dinner that night. The meal consisted of Khabili rice, an Afghan dish made with pistachios, almonds and cumin, allspice, and chicken cooked to perfection in a delicious spicy sauce. This time Lela didn't have to fight for food. There was plenty of it. We ate as much as we could, and then we rested for a little bit. Before we knew it, it was time for us to leave for the airport.

We felt bad for Sofia and her kids, as we had to leave them behind. They had to wait for their paperwork to go to Germany. (They actually ended up going the same route as we did to Germany, a couple of weeks later). Once we got to the airport, we were stopped from getting on the plane, since we did not have visas. We had round-trip tickets to visit Turkey and come back, but the person who got us the tickets failed to mention that we needed visas – the most important element. We had to spend that night at the airport, sleeping on the chairs. We were crying that night, and were so distraught.

We spent another couple of days in a hotel in Islamabad. Every day, we kept going to the Turkish embassy and waiting all day to get our visas, which was not very easy to do. They kept making excuses and wanted money. After 2-3 days, we did manage to get our visas. This time we left Pakistan for good.

~ Thirteen ~

Freedom

We flew into Istanbul, Turkey and took a cab to a hotel. All of a sudden, the air felt so fresh. We kept looking out the window at a whole, new world. People appeared free – walking, driving and shopping and so on. Even though we stayed in a hotel that had one bathroom on each end of the hall, we at least had running water. We even had a sink in our rooms.

The man who purchased the tickets for us in Pakistan told us to go to this hotel – it was part of the smuggler's network. At this hotel, we would find our next contact. He was an Afghan man in his late sixties, whose name could only be translated as, "14-year-old" (no joking). We thought a 14-year-old boy was coming, and we were confused. When he arrived he offered us his deal: "I'll give you round trip tickets to Germany, at double the price, leaving tomorrow." That's how the smugglers did it – they didn't want to keep us in any one place for very long.

By this time, Zaman was fed up with these people and their expensive deals, especially since we didn't have any money left. He told him, "We don't have that much money. We would like to talk to more people." The guy gave us some names of other connections, but they weren't any better. Zaman said, "No. I just don't want to do this anymore. And we don't have enough money, anyway." Zaman wanted to do the right thing. He wanted to go through the immigration and refugee process.

The next day, we all took the bus downtown to the Immigration and Refugee Office. We met Madam and her husband, who were from Geneva and ran the office. First Madam spoke to Zaman, and then to Ria and me. She spoke English with a French accent and was pale, in her sixties, pretty and very delicate. She fell in love with the children. But for some reason, she thought we would not qualify for refugee services.

"You cannot be approved for refugee application. You'll have to find some other way," she said. Zaman was very disappointed. Ria and I were both crying. We were about to leave, and Madam's husband opened the door for us. Suddenly, something made Madam and her husband change their minds – something about baby Aisal and 3-year-old Lela. Aisal was such a beautiful and happy baby, and Lela was so playful and curious. Madam saw our fear and disappointment. She called us back in.

"We will start your application process, but we still cannot promise anything," she said. Ria and I felt we could finally breathe the fresh air of Istanbul again. But Zaman was hesitant.

"I'm not sure if our case will go through," he worried.

~~~

The day finally came when we were taken to our interview. We were transported in a windowless van to an underground Interpol station. It was a very secretive operation. We spent the entire day there, and it was really scary. Each of the adults was interviewed separately for at least an hour or more. They asked us, "Why did you leave? What happened?" We told them the truth: "We were being harassed and followed, and our lives were in danger." The kids were getting restless and so were Ria, Zaman, and I. Finally, when all was said and done, our political refugee case was approved and the decision was made. We were accepted as refugees.

They said, "We can give you an option of which country you want to go to: Canada, Australia or America." We were like, "Are you kidding us?" We could not believe we were being given those choices. We never had choices in our lives ever – let alone anything like this.

Our answer was, "The USA, of course!"

It took the entire day to finish the paperwork and make us official. They took our pictures, fingerprints, gave us inoculations and took chest X-rays for tuberculosis, and all of the other necessary data. We were again packed up and hidden into the Interpol van, and that very evening, we were taken straight to the refugee camp, located in the suburbs of Istanbul.

We arrived at the camp, which was a gated, two-story building that held about fifty other people, most of whom were with their families. The building looked like it had been a school once upon a time. They gave us a big room with two bunk beds on the first floor. I had to sleep in the same room as the rest of my family until they found another room for me to share with a Russian woman and her 10-year-old son. The woman was not very happy that she had to share her room with me. She relaxed, though, once she found out that I was only going to sleep there, and that I would be spending most of my time downstairs with my family. I had been living with them for so long, I did not know how to do otherwise.

We found out that there were two other Afghan families in the camp. We quickly met them, as we longed for any contact with home, and visited them often at night. We would have tea and candy and chat about our lives and imagine what was going to happen. They had been there for 4-5 months already. They talked about how Madam came once a week to the camp for a visit, and how she brought goodies for everyone. "She assures us that our time will come," they told us.

As we explored more, it turned out that this camp also housed people from Romania, Czechoslovakia, and Russia. All of them were escaping from something and running to something better.

The camp was run by a supervisor and staff who gave us three meals a day in the cafeteria. They also offered English lessons three times a week, and Zaman went, though he was already pretty fluent in English. I still didn't feel comfortable in a classroom setting. Due to this (and my general shyness), I didn't participate much. I considered these my "reasons" for not participating. To justify this in my mind, I rationalized that my English was, "not that bad." Ria would join the class once in a while, but most of the time, she was extremely busy with the kids.

Some afternoons, we took the kids to a nearby park that had a playground. Other than that, we did not go out much, since we did not have any means of transportation or any money.

The tall gentleman from the refugee office would come on certain days to take us for our physicals and other paperwork. He did not talk much, though we could never figure out why. (We assumed that maybe he did not speak English, but then again, he didn't smile much either).

We liked to take the ferry from the Asian side of the city, where people were more conservative, to the European side, where everyone was wearing makeup and fancy clothes. We fixed egg sandwiches and ate them out on the balcony of the ferry. We couldn't leave the camp unless we had official permission; so we really enjoyed these trips whenever we could. The days were long, and we did not know how to keep ourselves occupied, so cabin fever set in quickly. We worried constantly about the future and what was going to happen to us, but we always stayed positive and tried to make the best of the situation.

Madam came every once in a while to the cafeteria, and people would gather and bustle around her like little butterflies, trying to make a good impression. They truly believed that she held their fates in her delicate hands, and if they treated her well, they could leave that much sooner.

Each floor had shared bathrooms. You had to either take a shower very early or very late not to be disturbed. This was especially a problem for us women, as the bathrooms were unisex and the last thing a young Afghan woman would ever want is to is go to Hell for having a man who was not her husband see her naked.

The food at the refugee camp was different, but was far better than what we lived on in Pakistan. As I have said, we mainly stayed in our room. The reasons for this were mostly due to the fact we felt "safer" there. Sadly, it was also that we didn't want to have to deal with "different" groups of people. In reality, we were very shy and reserved, and felt ashamed about living in a refugee camp. We did notice some other nationalities that were making friends and having fun, playing Ping-Pong and chess in the cafeteria. We truly wished that we could be like them, but since that was not the way we were raised, this did not happen. As a matter of fact, every time I thought of doing this, I saw a vision of my dad shaking his head at me, saying, "no."

~~~

Finally, after four months at the refugee camp, our visas came. But it turned out that we were now being sent to Italy – this was the second part of the refugee process. We went shopping the very next day. We bought some clothes for the children and for us to wear to the airport. Ria and I always bought the same style of clothes, just different colors: my dress was light blue with spaghetti straps, with a white jacket with blue trim. Ria's dress was lavender. Even though we were sisters-in-law, we were actually just sisters, and I was so grateful for this. We were so proud of our clothes and ecstatic about the trip.

The two Afghan families from the camp came to the airport to say goodbye to us. They were crying. We could not tell whether this was because they were going to miss us and were sad, or because they were still waiting for their visas, even though they arrived at the camp before we did.

~ Fourteen ~

Italy

We arrived at the airport in Rome, Italy and we were promptly greeted by a group of young men. They turned out to be Afghan refugees themselves. They welcomed us and said they were going to help us. We were impressed and again felt a little less "lost," since it was obvious that we were not the first ones to have made this journey.

In Italy, we were immediately put up in apartments in a city called Ostia Antica. We lived in the apartments for a month or so. We shared the one kitchen and bathroom in the hallway with other tenants. We were very happy about the living arrangements. We had gained some independence and were feeling more secure by the moment.

One day, reality came crashing down on us. Lela fell off a shopping cart in the grocery store, and she split her tongue. Blood was gushing all over, and Ria had to rush her to the hospital. Luckily, she just needed a few stitches and everything was OK. This was the first time we had something like this happen to the kids throughout our entire journey, and suddenly we were reminded that we were mortal once again.

Then, I had the misfortune of a toothache, and I went to the dentist. Instead of treating it or referring me to another dentist, the dentist just pulled my tooth out. The simple reason for this was that I could not communicate with anyone, and not one person there spoke a word of English. This was an easy way of getting rid of my pain.

There was a small group of Afghan men that lived in a villa across from the beach, and they became good friends with us. They actually agreed to vacate that house for us and found bedding and furniture for us that people had put out on the street. They were such good guys. We could not afford to purchase anything but groceries and rent.

We traveled once a month to Rome to get our welfare checks. We would pack up the entire family and just "go." On the train, we would see college kids kissing and getting into R-rated "performances" with each other. I was too embarrassed to look at them; we were not used to this type of behavior in any way (in fact, back home this would be reason for a lashing). We enjoyed riding the train to Rome on those days, as it felt like true freedom. We could not believe that you could get somewhere so fast, and it made our heads spin.

~~~

After moving into the house, we were introduced to a friendly neighbor who had two kids. Her husband was mostly out of town (we later found out she had some male "friends" too when her husband wasn't home). She invited us for dinner one night, and fixed a roasted chicken dinner with potatoes and carrots and Italian vegetables. It was the best meal that we had had since leaving home, and we savored every bite. That was the only Italian friend we had.

The area we lived in was not a very safe part of town. Some of the teenage kids living near the beach were wild, and they would snatch women's purses off their shoulders. We constantly had to watch our purses, and never carried them on our shoulders. Men had to carry their money in an inside shirt pocket (they actually had shirts especially made just for this reason).

We came home one day after going grocery shopping (which we always did as a family) to find a sight we had never encountered in our entire lives. We were very shocked to find the door open and our clothes spread all over the hallway. Our one suitcase containing all the clothes we had was open, the one little bag of change we had was gone, and some of our valuables had disappeared.

Our neighbor called the police. The police came and wrote a report, and left. They didn't speak English, and our neighbor spoke to them in Italian. We didn't know what just happened. We thought the police were going to catch the thieves right away and recover our belongings. Needless to say, we never heard from the police again, nor did we ever see our precious, few belongings again.

For the rest of our stay at the villa, we lived in constant fear. One day, we were having lunch in the kitchen dining area when I was startled again. I was sitting across from my bedroom when I saw the wooden blinds (which had been latched closed from the inside of my window) move. I saw a hand slide inside to open the latch on the window in the middle of the day. I jumped up, yelling *Ladro! Ladro! Ladro!* I didn't know much Italian, however, I did know that "*ladro*" meant, "thief." I scared the thief away, but that one incident made Ria and me become paranoid. For weeks, we stayed up all night looking out the window, holding our little vegetable peeling knife. We didn't sleep much anymore. Zaman and the kids were the only ones who slept.

Some evenings, we went to a small amusement park with the kids and enjoyed watching them riding the rides. If they behaved,

Zaman got them ice cream. Ria and I went window-shopping a lot. We visited other Afghans and socialized some. We were all so frustrated, because we did not know when we were going to get our US visas. Rumors were spreading around that no one was getting visas anymore, and we were going to be deported. As a result, Zaman was getting anxious, and in the process was making Ria and me nervous too. A couple months later, the other two Afghan families that we met in the refugee camp in Istanbul also came to Italy. We visited each other and often shared meals and tea.

We were all more independent in Italy. We went to the Vatican once for a tour and had a picnic. We enjoyed that day a lot. People were roller skating and having a good time. We were amazed at how carefree and alive they were. We were so shy; we never just went and sat on the beach. And Zaman would have killed me if I spoke to an Italian man. So, of course that thought never crossed my mind.

We ended up living in Italy for six months. Finally, our visas arrived. We had actually just moved to Lido di Ostia, and into a new apartment. Because the office didn't know our new address, the other Afghan families had to come looking for us to tell us that our visas had arrived.

Once again, the two Afghan families said goodbye to us at the airport, and they were crying. Zaman, Ria, the kids and I were all dressed up in suits. After all we had been through, this was the trip we had been dreaming of; the one we had been waiting for a whole year, and the trip where we finally got a sponsor. This was our future and destiny. This is what we had wanted all along, to come to America, to the land of freedom, where we did not have to worry about war, camps, or *ladros* anymore.

~ Fifteen ~

Rhode Island

We wanted to look our best, because now we were going to America. We wore our three-piece suits that we had purchased in Italy – the only suits we owned – with matching skirts, vests and jackets. For a brief moment we forgot the fact that we were still refugees, and that our sponsors were waiting for Afghan refugees. We knew that they had never had refugees from Afghanistan, but that they knew some Afghan families in the area, and were actually very close to them. They were familiar with some of the Afghan traditions, and were ready to be the family – and the bridge – that we needed for our new lives.

It was September 1981. We arrived at the New York airport at night. I don't remember which airport, but it took us quite a while to go through immigration. It was a little scary, because they had to check all of our papers and make sure everything was legal. There were other refugees who were going through at the same time, and that made it seem a little better. But we saw them being questioned too, and we were worried that we could be sent back.

We then flew in a very small twelve-passenger plane to Rhode Island. This plane, compared to the large international 707 plane we were on before, was making the family and me a little nervous.

We could feel all the turbulence and movement, every little bump, twist and grind. It was making me sick. We could see the pilot and everyone. That is when I realized a great truth in life: sometimes it's better not to be able to see the pilot.

When we finally got to the little airport in Rhode Island, a tall woman with short hair picked us up. She was a friend of our sponsors. There was no way that we thought she was Afghan, until the moment that she started speaking Farsi (our native language) with an American accent.

"Salaam alaikum," she said. Our eyes bulged.

"Oh, are you Afghan?" we asked.

"Yes, what did you think I was?"

"We thought you were American!" Her name was Farzana, and she drove us for about an hour until we arrived at the designated spot: our sponsors' big two-storey, brick home. It was about 10 pm, and Mr. and Mrs. L were waiting for us. They had expected to see a couple with three little children, and definitely not a well-dressed group in suits. Mrs. L came outside in her nightgown and was so surprised; she clasped her hands over her mouth when she saw us. Somehow, she thought that I would be a baby, not an adult. We were probably listed as a couple with three kids in the immigration process. She had fixed up the downstairs for us to sleep in, and she had a crib for "the baby." Instead, she had to give me her son's bed to sleep in that night (she told us that story later on, and it was so funny). We all slept peacefully. We felt at home.

Mrs. L was a kind, soft-spoken woman with fair skin and blond hair. Mr. L was a quiet man, a physics professor at the University of Rhode Island. They had sponsored people from other countries before. However, as Mrs. L told us later, no one quite like us. "You looked like diplomats that first night you arrived, with your matching suits on," she said. She took us for our immigration paperwork the next day. Then she immediately took us job-hunting and oriented us around the town of Kingston, Rhode Island. Mr. and Mrs. L lived near the beach, but the beach was cold. Kingston was a small and quiet town, where everybody knew everybody – a university town with a young crowd. Everyone was so friendly, and our sponsors were very intelligent. We felt calm for the first time in months.

Farzana, the tall Afghan woman who met us at the airport, happened to have a big family in town. They had lived there for quite a while. Her husband taught at the university, and so did she. They had kids and a very large extended family. Her sister-in-law, Sureena, also lived with them. She had recently emigrated from Afghanistan with her mother. Sureena was around Ria's and my age, and we quickly became good friends. Sureena, Ria and I learned to ride bicycles (though I had a bit of a leg-up on them). We went to the government center to learn English on a regular basis, and we were anxious to fit in.

Mrs. L took me for my first job interview to work as an RN at the local hospital. I naively thought I could easily get a job as a nurse-midwife. I came to find out that it would be very complicated. I had to get my transcripts first, and then send them to the Commission on Graduates of Foreign Nursing Schools office in New York. Then, if approved, I would have to take the CGFNS exam. If I passed that, I could then take the state board exam and pass the test to get my license to practice as an RN. After all of that, if I wanted to practice as a midwife, I needed to go to back to school to get my certification as a midwife. Later on, when I found out what "transcript" meant, I knew there was no way I could request mine. The nursing school was not going to send my transcripts. After all, I'd escaped my country and become a political refugee; so how could I request official records? My sponsor said that she knew someone that owned a nursing home, and suggested that I could work as a nurse's aide while I gathered up my paperwork for schooling.

Mrs. L took me for an interview as a nurse's aide, and I did far better with this one. The job was not as detailed, and I was hired right away. I was very excited. Ria started volunteering at a daycare and taking her kids with her. Zaman was doing some odd jobs to make some money, and he started going to school at the same time, studying to become a librarian. We were able to rent our own home within just a couple of weeks. I had my own bedroom, and even the kids had their own bedrooms. I felt like a princess, with my own closet and a little window. Everyone was settling down for the time being.

I started working in a privately owned forty-bed nursing home. At the beginning, I was shocked that all these elderly residents had been abandoned by their families. I felt very sorry for them, because where I came from, families took care of their parents better. They were cared for by all of the family. Our elders were the decision-makers and they had more authority within the family, even long past their productive years.

It made me think of my own mother. We took such good care of her. My sister had actually changed her life's course forever, in order to stay with my mother and take care of her. Zaybah and I used to help her bathe, and shampoo, brush and braid her long hair. We made sure she wore nice, clean clothes and looked and felt good at all times. We loved her, and we knew she had a hard life, and it was time for her to enjoy and live a little easier. Thinking this way, I suddenly missed my mother. I wished she was with me, and so I wrote to her and told her about this and every other feeling that was in my heart.

I worked hard at the nursing home. Most residents were

dependent and needed help with everything. Working all day lifting, toileting, bathing, feeding, and putting them back to bed took so much out of me, though. I was emotionally and physically exhausted.

I never missed a day at work. In September 1981, I was making about $3.50 an hour at my first job. It was enough to pay my tuition for a couple of classes at the community college, provided that I lived for free with my brother.

All of a sudden, I found myself becoming more American when Zaman taught both Ria and me how to drive. Then I drove every morning to work with Zaman sitting next to me. We had an older, used car that we could afford. After getting off work, I would either take the bus home or have one of my co-workers take me home.

I made friends at work and enjoyed their company. Sometimes they laughed at my pronunciation of words. They never knew how uncomfortable and truly embarrassed that made me feel, and I did not know how to laugh with them. After all, I only knew how to be perfect and never make a mistake. I learned the phrase, "Everyone makes mistakes." Only in America could people get away with such a saying. Where I am from, it's a very different story.

I had been invited to a Christmas party at a co-worker's house. I was trying to be proper and friendly, and I decided to go. I couldn't understand why this one man kept talking to me and why he was interested in what I was saying.

The next day when I went to work, they asked me, "How was your blind date?" But I didn't know what they were talking about.

"What's a blind date?" I asked. "The person wasn't blind. Or did I miss it?" After my co-worker explained it to me, I was about to die. If I had known, I wouldn't have gone in the first place, or ever talked to that man. Girls from my country didn't date at all, at least not in public – never mind a blind date.

In Afghanistan, there were some girls who dated in secret, without their parents' knowledge. Those girls were usually not considered to be "good girls" according to tradition, and they had a few other names for them, which can't be mentioned here (or anywhere else in civilized company, for that matter). Most Afghan mothers don't want brides like that for their sons. My mom always told us, "Be reserved and proper when you are out in public." We didn't talk to anyone – especially men.

So, since I was new to the States, I had to learn a mountain of information in a short period of time, all while enduring culture shock around every corner. I knew, though, that I couldn't follow this liberated culture. Due to my respect for my family and the way I was raised, I knew my mother and father (and especially my brother Zaman) would never approve of such a thing. We were too new to the culture. Even though I had the pleasure of spending some time in Santa Cruz during my nursing program, we were never exposed to anything like dating. The coordinators made sure that we stayed within our Afghan cultural rules and traditions, and also that we were never exposed to situations like I suddenly found myself in now.

Zaman and Ria worked hard to take care of things. Ria was hired at the day care where she had been volunteering for the past three months. She took the kids with her, which was a major convenience. On weekends, we browsed the yard sales and went shopping in the afternoons. We cooked our meals at home and enjoyed our time when we were at home. Occasionally, we did go out with our coworkers, but we were always cautious, as we did not ever want to embarrass ourselves, our sponsors or our families half a world away.

Mrs. L, our sponsor, was always there for us, even after we moved out. On Halloween, she took us trick-or-treating. She prepared Thanksgiving dinner for us. It was the best roast turkey that we ever had, with mashed potatoes, stuffing, salad and dessert. She took us to a Christmas program at her church. She introduced us to her friends and family. We were intrigued by the Christian holidays and really enjoyed celebrating the American traditions with our sponsors and American friends. We celebrated all of our Muslim holidays, too, with the tall lady's Afghan family and our sponsor. We shared both old and new traditions with everyone. Mrs. L often said, "I am so proud of my refugee family, for working so hard and trying to make up for everything they have lost or never known." The opportunities and the things available for us to learn were endless.

In Rhode Island, November 1981. I'm wearing the suit that we purchased in Italy.

~ Sixteen ~

No Last Goodbyes

Two years passed. I kept writing to my mother and I managed to send her little gifts on Mother's Day or the Eids (Muslim religious holidays). I was even thinking how I could try to get my mother to come to America. My oldest brother, Amir, always wrote what my mother was saying or doing, and that she missed us a lot or that she wanted us to write more.

Suddenly and without warning, he didn't write much. Or when he did write, he didn't say what she was doing anymore. One time, all he wrote was that, "Her arthritic bones do not hurt anymore." As I finished reading that letter, I was upset, but I could not understand why. Zaman had handed the letter to me after he read it, and he had been crying for a couple of hours.

I kept on reading the letter over and over again and could not put it down. When my brain finally allowed me to really "read" the letter, I understood that it said she was resting in peace. Our mother had actually died a year before, of a heart attack at the age of fifty-seven.

Amir wrote in the letter that he just couldn't bear to tell us, because he didn't want to upset us. He knew that we weren't going to be able to come anyway, and did not want us to worry so much about our mother. He finished the letter by assuring us that she was fine, that she is in heaven and that she will watch over us. I had a hard time finishing the letter. Zaman was holding me, and we were sobbing together. All of a sudden, I felt so alone in the world. I remembered the day we left Kabul, and my mother saying to us, "This is my last goodbye." I had not understood what she was saying at the time, but suddenly I did. I had never thought of my mother dying. I had never considered it for a second. That is something no one wants to think about, and I had not – could not – not *my* mother.

I got in my car and drove to the quiet beach. No one was there that afternoon. I started walking and screaming at the top of my lungs. I had never done that as an adult. I cried as loud as I could. I was upset for not knowing, and I felt betrayed. I felt like I was not important enough to be informed. I could have grieved with my family, even if I couldn't go. Why, oh why, couldn't I have been allowed to grieve at the proper time?

It turned out that the night before my mother died, she had some chest pain, and Zaybah gave her some of her medicine. Zaybah wanted to take her to the hospital, but Mom declined, saying that she wanted to stay home. After she took her medicine, she slept really well, Zaybah remembers. The next day, she told Zaybah that she was feeling better and told her to go to work. My father came to visit her that morning, which he did sometimes. My mother and father still had a lot of respect for each other, even though he lived with Zewar. They had tea together. After he left, Mom got up to make dough for bread, as per her normal morning routine.

Amir's wife was living across the hall. She heard some noise, and when she came to check on Mom, she was lying on the floor gasping for air and her mouth was foaming. Amir's wife called for help. By the time help arrived, though, Mom's heart had stopped. She passed away. *Mami* died just the way she always wanted. She had told us that she hoped that when her time came, she would have a fever the night before and an easy death the next morning. That is what she prayed for all her life. She did not want to be dependent on anyone. God granted her wish.

I thought of Zaybah, my poor sister who had stayed behind. We didn't have any communication by phone, and the letters didn't come that often, maybe once a month. What was she going to do? Or better yet, what had happened to her already?

Zaybah was alone after my mother passed away. She got married a year later to a pharmacist; the marriage was arranged by one of her friends. Amir, my oldest brother, gave her a nice wedding. I was glad she had someone in her life now, since she had been taking care of Mom and working night shifts at the hospital. She has always been a caring soul. Zaybah moved to the Province of Lugar, about fifty miles from Kabul. She now took on the care of her aging mother-in-law and father-in-law. She had to learn the countryside traditions and customs. She stayed home and took care of everyone. When she had a baby, there was no transportation to the clinic or doctor. A home-trained midwife delivered the baby, and Zaybah almost bled to death.

Amir went to visit her at times, and he could not believe all the hard work she did. Zaybah reminded him of our mother, and it broke his heart to see her like that. The one redeeming factor in this was that her husband was a very nice man who truly loved her.

I felt guilty for leaving Zaybah behind, and I made myself take all the blame for how Zaybah's life had turned out. I cried for a long time. I felt like no one understood my pain – the pain of losing my mother. I felt sad for not being able to give my mother all the things I wanted her to have. I also felt that she had been cheated of all the love I would never get to express to her. I wanted to say to my mother, "I love you," and, "Yes, I did have the best mother in the world."

Somehow, it was easier to say that now, but it was too late. I thought of how I panicked every time she hurt. And how I would hold the holy Quran to my chest, and pray that she would be OK. The worst feeling of all, though, was that I could not tell her goodbye.

We had a memorial service with the other Afghan family in town, and my aunt Sofia and her family. My aunt was actually living close to us again at this time. Sofia had left Germany after her 19-year-old daughter died of complications from a minor surgical procedure. They had moved to Arizona, lived there for a couple years, and then finally moved close to us in Rhode Island.

There were strong connections between our two families, because of everything we had gone through together. Sofia was still grieving for her daughter, but her husband and three teenage sons always supported her. Sometimes I thought about how hard things were on her family, and how all these years had been so tough on all of us.

I dreamed about my mother all the time. My mother was always alive in my dreams, smiling at me, as if she were truly happy and at peace. I felt better whenever I would see her in my dreams. However, during the day when I remembered my mother, I would sometimes cry uncontrollably. My heart simply ached for her.

~~~

Two years after my mom's death, my father died of pneumonia. This time Amir only waited 2-3 months to tell us. Again, both Zaman and I went through the grieving process and all of the guilty feelings for not having been there for him. And above all, we suffered for never having gotten the chance to tell our father that we loved him, and to say goodbye before he died. We were estranged, due to the fact that he lived with his new wife and kids. We still loved him and cared for him, though.

Now that we were so far away, my feelings were much stronger for my family back home. We had a memorial service for my father with my aunt Sofia, her family and a few friends. I truly believed that my mother and father were together now in heaven. Nothing and nobody was going to separate them, and on that note, I felt better, and life went on.

~ Seventeen ~

Getting Married

I decided that it was time for me to concentrate on everything else in life. When I was nineteen years old, I had planned to be married by age twenty-five, and have a baby by the age of twenty-six. Otherwise, according to Afghan culture, I would be too old. Too old to have children or to even find a husband, because men prefer to marry young girls.

I started panicking when I turned twenty-five. I suddenly realized just how old I had become with no husband. I could not date because of my strict upbringing. This of course made it very hard to find a husband.

In 1984, we all moved to Alexandria, Northern Virginia for better jobs and better opportunities that come with living in a bigger city. After a couple years, I did go on some dates with Middle Eastern men, but they did not go well at all. The men did not want to be seen dating me in public, due to the fact that they wanted to save their faces and mine (or so they would say). I did not appreciate that, and the dates ended quickly.

I wanted to be treated like a normal woman and be respected for who I was, not just because I was Afghan. One date wanted me to duck my head down in his car as we passed by other Afghans. That was the last straw. By this time, it had been five years since we came to the US as refugees, and I was becoming a little Americanized.

I was still struggling to take classes and complete my transcripts for the CGFNS exam. I started working in a nursing home in Northern Virginia, but it seemed like my qualifications were only good enough for that. My hourly rate was about $4.00, which did not pay for anything except my classes at the community college.

I still lived with my brother, though it felt like (and I was treated like) I was one of the kids. Zaman and Ria were working hard to pay for an apartment and meet their daily needs. I felt bad for being such a burden. I took care of the kids as much as I could, and helped with chores and some of the expenses, but in my heart, it was not enough. Sometimes I wished I could live with some of my friends, but that was not acceptable to Zaman and Ria.

At one point, Zaman got a very good offer to work in Saudi Arabia. He declined it though, because he did not want to leave me behind. My only wish was that I would not be such a responsibility for them and could be free on my own.

On the work front, I got tired of working at the nursing home. If you have ever worked in a nursing home, you know just how tough that job is. All day long, you must physically pick up patients who cannot move, take care of their basic needs and speak for them when they cannot speak for themselves. It is truly rewarding work for the soul, but pure torture on the body.

I applied at some of the high-end department stores, including Woodward & Lothrop. I actually got hired, and was put to work in the junior department with Mariam, another Afghan girl. We instantly became good friends. We had some really good times – going to the gym, walking, running and eating and just hanging out together.

During a lunch break, we were talking about guys.

"I'll never find a husband or get married," I told her.

"I have a friend named Dean. He lives in Omaha, Nebraska. I think you should get to know him," she said. Actually he was a friend of Mariam's brothers, and Dean kept in close contact with Mariam because he liked her. But Mariam already had an American boyfriend, which seemed odd to me. I couldn't believe how bold it was for an Afghan woman to have an American boyfriend.

"What does Dean look like?"

"He seems like a good guy, very nice and funny, just a regular Afghan guy," she said.

I agreed to correspond with him. So I called him and we talked on the phone for a while and exchanged pictures. When I got his picture, I was not sure what to think about him. He looked a little older, and prideful, unlike other Afghan men; though I just could not quite put my finger on why, exactly.

We continued to talk on the phone, and I found out that he had lived next to my aunt's neighbor in Kabul. Even though we had lived in Kabul not too far from each other, I had never met him. Mariam spoke highly of him, so I was intrigued. I figured this might be as good a chance for independence from my family as I would get, so I decided to take a leap of faith.

My family made arrangements for him to come to Virginia to meet me at my brother's house. My first impression of him made me a bit nervous, although I could not figure out why he made me nervous. After awhile, we spoke by ourselves and I learned that he lived by himself. He had immigrated to Germany as a refugee and then to Omaha where his sponsor lived. He had many Afghan friends in Omaha, because there were many Afghans living in the Midwest at that time.

His American sponsor and Afghan friends were constantly asking him when he was going to get married, because, after all, he was in his late thirties. They thought he needed to settle down. His father, like my father, had also married a second wife, and Dean had a large step family. He was the only member of his family who completed his high school education, and he was the only one who left Afghanistan.

Dean was the youngest of his brothers and had a younger sister. He said, "My oldest brother was abusive to me, and wanted me to work on the family farm and obey him without question." So, Dean would sneak out to school after doing his chores. If his brother found out, he would beat him up. Dean seemed very independent and confident, but at the same time, very mistrusting of others in the world.

The next day, Dean came to talk with me. We went to Mt. Vernon Park, and talked with each other for a few minutes. Then he spoke with my family by the waterfront. He told me that he was ready to settle down, and that he wanted a permanent relationship.

"I want to settle down with an Afghan girl, somebody who is educated and has a job." Dean said he liked "my quiet manner." I, on the other hand, didn't feel too comfortable with him. I thought to myself, "If he likes me, that is all that matters, since it is going to be a traditional Afghan marriage. You have to make the best out of it, no matter what happens in the end."

"I am open-minded and you can continue going to school and working while you're married," he said. I felt confused and didn't know why we were moving so fast.

"I need to take some time and think about it," I told him. I didn't even know this man, but I was willing to take the time to get to know him and give him a chance.

Dean was persistent and very persuasive. He was not the man of my dreams, and I didn't want to marry the first person who showed an interest in me. Dean told me to think about his marriage proposal.

We went home, and Ria wanted to know what was said. By this time, I had begun to really think about his proposal. I thought if I marry this man, it might turn out to be a good thing. After all, he was not a typical Afghan man who would make me stay home to cook and clean. I would have my own home and wouldn't have to continue living with my brother for the rest of my life. After living with them for six years, I felt very close to Ria, and I knew that Zaman, my brother loved me. Although my brother was very good to me, I just wanted to have my own life, and I wanted his family to have their privacy.

I come from a good family. *Mami* always said, "My family is descended from Mohammed Zahi; we are very sophisticated people with strong morals." Her family was Tajik, originated from Tajikistan, and they were Sunnis. I wanted to keep this tradition, and the family name, by getting married, even if I did not feel any attraction to this man.

It was time for me to make my decision to accept or reject Dean's proposal. He would be going back to Omaha and wanted an answer before he left. My family and I said, "Yes," and gave him a bag of candy, which, in the Afghan tradition, signifies the acceptance of a marriage proposal. Dean expressed his happiness and headed back to Omaha.

Honestly, I was very scared and nervous to marry Dean. However, in keeping with Afghan tradition, here I was, twenty-eight years old now, getting married to someone I barely knew let alone loved.

~~~

Dean called occasionally, and we spoke, but I didn't feel like I could really open up to him, because we didn't have much in common. At times, I found him to be loud when he talked on the phone. It sounded like he was yelling. When I told him about it, he got upset and truly yelled. I got worried and told Ria, "This is not going to work." Ria contacted him about his loud and rude behavior. He apologized and said he didn't mean to yell at me. After that, he was nicer when we talked on the phone.

After a couple of months, he said that the next time he came to see my family and me, he wanted an official engagement party. So, Ria gave us a traditional engagement party with the family and some friends. I wore a beautiful, baby blue, long dress with a high, lace collar and long sleeves, in a size six. I wore blue and pearl earrings to match, and if I don't mind saying so, I looked beautiful! However, I did not feel beautiful, because, I was so nervous. My shoulders were riding up to my ears, and I forced a fake smile for everyone there to see. Dean, however, appeared very happy as he laughed and danced, and ate up the tray of decorated engagement candy and goodies that Ria put together for the party.

Dean and I spent a couple of days together with the family. I did feel a little more connection to him in person rather than over the phone. We went to the park and other public places. We tried to talk about things and find common ground. Most of the time, when Dean tried to kiss me, I felt uncomfortable and not attracted to him. I hadn't kissed a man before. But by the time I drove him to the airport the day he was leaving, I felt a little sad when he held me tight and told me he would be back.

Dean was anxious to get married so he wouldn't have to keep coming back to Virginia all the time to court me. He wanted me to come to Omaha with him so that we could spend a week or so together. I told him no, because according to Afghan tradition, we were not supposed to be together in his home before marriage. We decided to get married sooner, so that we could be together and get to know each other. We set the wedding date.

My lovely sister-in-law Ria helped me with the wedding plans, and Zaman took care of the venue, meal, and music. Ria and I purchased the wedding dress and wedding ring. Against tradition, Dean told me to go choose my own wedding ring and band the way I liked it, and to buy him a band that matched. I took out a loan for the wedding sets. Dean came the day before the wedding to try on the suit we bought him, and the ring, and they fit perfectly.

We didn't have a lot of money, so we rented a party room in a friend's apartment complex, and rented tables and chairs for the guests. We hired an Afghan chef to prepare the hors d'oeuvres and dinner. Typically, in Afghan culture, the groom's side pays for most of the expenses and arranges the ceremony and reception. Although it didn't seem fair that Dean was not following Afghan tradition regarding the wedding preparations, all I had my sights on at the time was becoming a bride-to-be.

~~~

On the day of the wedding, I went by myself to have my hair done at the JC Penney hair salon. They washed my shoulder-length hair and styled it nicely. But, the wind was so strong that day, that it unraveled my new style. I remembered the day my oldest sister got married. She must have had five or six women with her at the hair salon, and we had so much fun. Suddenly, I missed my mother and sisters and I started crying. Things did not get better, because when I got into my car, I saw that my gas tank was on empty. As I was getting gas,

I dropped the gas cap on the ground, and it rolled under the car. I then had to crawl under the car to get it. Here I was, given one thing to do, while my brother and sister-in-law were handling everything else, and I felt like a total failure.

Next, I needed to go to my friend's apartment to get ready while she was at work. I applied my makeup and put on my wedding dress. I looked at myself in the mirror: I looked beautiful in that ivory, satin long-sleeved, lacy high-collared dress, and I was proud of how I looked.

Before Zaman and Ria made it to the party room, the guests had already arrived, and were waiting to be let in. Once things got started, and the music was playing, suddenly everything looked beautiful. As I walked down the aisle with my aunt and Ria, my friends held the holy Quran over my head. I was shaking, and was so self-conscious as all the guests were watching us walk down the aisle. This was not one of my favorite moments; not like I imagine most young women fantasize about.

During the ceremony, the elders of the family were present. A shawl was held over our heads, with a mirror underneath, and we looked up at the mirror and into other's eyes. Then we read a verse from the Holy Quran together. Next, we fed each other the *moleeda*, the dry sweet, buttery, crumbled bread. This was followed by giving each other a sip of juice from a glass. Then we put henna into the palms of our hands, and wrapped our hands with a glittery fabric that Ria made especially for the ceremony. Over the next few hours, the henna would stain our hands red, and this would supposedly bring good luck and a happy marriage.

The actual legal ceremony had taken place early that morning at the Mullah's house. I was wearing a green dress, which is the color of luck, for the *nickah*, or agreement. The Mullah read a verse from the Quran, and then he asked Dean and me three times if we agreed to be married. My family and two male cousins witnessed the signature and the event. This was more open than most Afghan ceremonies, where the witnesses usually go behind the curtain to talk to the bride, and then they bring the message to Mullah to verify the agreement.

After the ceremony, I was sitting next to Dean on the couch that was set up for us on the stage. I tried to keep calm and talk to people that kept coming up to congratulate us.

Dean had invited some of his friends from New York to the wedding, and during the reception they were dancing and carrying on with themselves. Of course, they were the only ones drinking alcohol, as this was not the way we were raised to behave. My dear brother, Zaman, did not appreciate them acting like that at all. He just stood in a corner, appearing very bothered and upset. After all, he was the brother – the only brother at that time to see his sister get married and leave his home. He had taken care of me for the past six years like one of his own children. This was the promise he made to my mother and father. Now he was not sure how this was going to turn out. So far, he was not happy with Dean, because he didn't put much effort into me, or the wedding.

The wedding party was over at around midnight. Ria and Zaman had rented a hotel room for us newlyweds in Falls Church, Virginia, and it was set up with brand new sheets and a comforter for its purity. Some of my family members took us there and made sure everything was OK before they left.

That night, I did not feel comfortable consummating my marriage with Dean. I felt very uneasy and scared. I wished for something to put me to sleep rather than have to go through this part of the wedding night. Dean was patient though, and he said, "I can wait."

The next morning my aunt Sofia came to visit, and I was glad
to see her. But I was too embarrassed to tell her about what had
happened the night before.

We went back to my brother's home to spend a couple days
with them. Then I packed up all my stuff into a 1986 Nissan Sentra
and headed off to Omaha with my new husband, Dean. It was
so hard to say goodbye to my brother, Ria and the kids. We all
had brunch at Big Boy's restaurant that morning and I remember
looking back from the car, watching Ria crying hard. We had grown
close all those years.

We drove all day to Indiana, spent the night there and the next
morning we were on the road again. We had plenty of time to talk
and get to know each other. We talked about our families, home
and everything else. I could not shake my sense of unease, though.
After a while, I started crying and did not know what to do, because
I was going somewhere I had never been, to live with a husband I
did not know or fully understand. The flat scenery and long drive
made me reflect on how I had left my family and home once again.
It was upsetting to me, and I felt guilty for not being a good wife.
I thought there was something wrong with me since I still had not
consummated my marriage with him.

Finally, after traveling for two whole days, we arrived at his
one bedroom apartment on the second floor. I noticed how it was
decorated according to his tastes, not mine. It was nice to see the
plants that he had all over the apartment. There was some food
prepared by his best friend for us to eat, which was good, since we
were starving.

Eventually I was able to sleep with Dean after about one week.
By then, my obligation as a wife had been met, and I was happy.

~ Eighteen ~

Zohra

I spent my days cleaning the apartment, washing clothes, cooking Afghan food, and entertaining his Afghan friends. His friends gave us a reception a few weeks after we got back to Omaha. But it felt odd to be the center of attention, and I felt anxious and self-conscious amongst fifty of his friends. They arranged everything and cooked all the food and we helped provide the financial obligations for our reception.

Dean introduced me to his favorite hobby by taking me to his dance club, where he enjoyed ballroom dancing. He introduced me to his dancing friends and I watched him dance with them. When I tried to dance, I'd sweat and get dizzy each time, especially when I was swing dancing. I felt bad that I could not dance.

Within a few weeks after our wedding, I began to feel nauseated all the time and dizzy. I could not stand the smell of food, especially meat, and could not eat, even if it was prepared in other people's house. I went to the doctor and found out I was pregnant. Dean and I were very excited to find out that I was pregnant so soon. We were ready for a baby and celebrated our joy together. I had always wanted to have a baby because I felt I had a lot of love to give.

By the end of the first trimester, I began to feel better. During this time, I started working in the labor and delivery department of the local hospital as a nurse's aide. This made me very tired, as I told my sister-in-law Ria. She invited me to visit her when I was about three months pregnant. Dean was working, so I went on the trip alone. I had a good visit with Zaman, Ria, and their kids.

When I returned to Omaha, I noticed right away that the wedding cake ornament with the ceramic birds had been placed in the bottom drawer of the dresser. I will never forget that feeling of betrayal; that Dean had been trying to hide something from me. When I asked him about it, he said, "I had a friend, a girl from dance class, over to visit and I did not want her to know I was married, because it is a ballroom club for singles and I get a discount that way." I was very suspicious and hurt, so I put the wedding cake ornament back where I had left it before I went on my trip.

~~~

Over time, I was left alone on Fridays and weekends, because I could not dance. Once, when I was about eight months pregnant, we went to Dean's friend's house for a visit. Then he went dancing afterwards. I was so angry at him for leaving me alone at this stage of my pregnancy and I had no way of reaching him if I needed him. At that time, I didn't have any friends of my own yet. So that night, I cried and felt so alone as I thought about Ria. She was my best friend, my confidante, and I missed her right now. When I told Dean the next day how upset I was, he responded by getting mad and telling me, "don't be such a crybaby."

Later on, he decided to take me on a camping trip with his friends during my thirty-ninth week of pregnancy. Ria kept calling the house, and when she couldn't reach me, she got very nervous, and tried the hospital. I called her when I returned and said everything was all right. She was concerned about me going camping that late in my pregnancy.

About two days after our camping trip, when I was thirty-nine and a half weeks pregnant, my water broke at 2 am. Fortunately, Dean was home, and he took me to the hospital. I was not in labor, but since my water broke, they had to keep me until l started labor the next day. Dean had to take a real estate test, so he left late that morning, and then left me alone again on the day I was in labor. The doctor gave me pain medication, so all I remember was waking up, disoriented, and then dozing off again, until finally I had the most beautiful little girl in my arms. She was born around 2 am and was stubborn from the very beginning; she had to be pulled out with forceps.

Dean was there, and he took many pictures. She weighed over eight pounds, and had my dark hair and big brown eyes. That night, I was feverish and exhausted, so I slept the whole night and throughout the following morning. When I awoke, I was surprised to see that Zaman, Ria and the kids had come to be there for us. We took Zohra, my new baby, home. I had the worst time trying to nurse her and calm her down. The next day, she developed jaundice. She turned yellow and I had to take her back to the hospital for phototherapy. I kept looking at my little baby, wearing an eye mask and no clothes in the small isolette with the blue lights. She was screaming and rolling from side to side. I couldn't help sobbing, and I was tortured thinking of my baby being trapped in there; I couldn't even hold her. Finally, one of the nurses came and assured me that she would be fine.

The next morning, the doctor said I could take her home. I was so happy to take her home and show her to my family. My niece and nephew were in awe at this new baby, and kept gathering around her to take a peek. I think it was Dean's idea to go to the park for a picnic.

I didn't feel too thrilled about going to the park with a newborn baby, but I couldn't argue about that in front of my brother and his family. I wrapped up my baby and covered her face and head. I was panicked at the thought of any bees coming close to the baby carrier. I was glad when we came home and the baby was safe.

Zaman, Ria and the kids left after a short stay, and I was alone again, staying home taking care of little Zohra. I fell into a pattern of cooking and cleaning. That is what I was now "supposed" to do. I was home all the time, never getting a break at all. Dean got breaks from the routine. He worked and came home with dinner ready, a clean house, and a baby – and then on weekends he went out dancing.

He was very religious around other Afghans – he read the Quran and prayed at memorial services – but he didn't pray or fast at home. I continued to feel lonely, and now Zohra was three months old. I decided that I needed to move closer to my family who would give me more support with childcare, because then I could get out of the house and work so that I could support Zohra and myself. Dean said, "If you move near your family, you'll be responsible for anything that goes wrong. If you do this, you'll have total responsibility for Zohra's care. And don't bother me, since you'll have your family to support you." I knew what I needed to do, so Dean and I packed everything and moved to my brother's home in Virginia. We lived in his basement, since neither one of us had jobs yet. At first, Dean had little success, but eventually he got hired at the Department of Motor Vehicles.

While a neighbor watched Zohra, I worked part time as a bank teller. We were making enough money to get our own place, but Dean didn't want to move yet. We all slept in the same room, and if Zohra woke up in the middle of the night, Dean would get angry with me.

I'll never forget one night when Zohra was so fussy. I tried everything to calm her down – putting her in the swing, rocking, and doing anything I could. But Dean said, "Don't get up, you'll spoil her, just let her cry herself to sleep." She kept crying and fussing. Dean got so angry that he picked up the swing set with Zohra in it and threw it across the room. I jumped out of bed and picked up my child from the swing set. I was so scared that he might get up and repeat the behavior or (heaven knows) what he might do to me. Fortunately he didn't get back up, and he went to sleep. I tried to put Zohra back to sleep, and she went to sleep quickly this time. I think she realized her dad was upset, even though she was only about 7-8 months old.

Finally, I got Dean to agree to find a place of our own, but he didn't act on it. Instead, he blamed me for having a job he didn't like. He blamed me for traffic, and not being able to have time to go out dancing. I decided that it was time to take matters into my own hands. One morning, I took Zohra with me apartment hunting. Unfortunately, most landlords did not want to rent to a woman with a child, so I spent the whole day searching without any success.

Dean went the next day and found a place for us to live. Finally, we had our own place, and I was very happy and excited for us. We bought second hand furniture and household goods. Zohra had her own bedroom, and we had our own kitchen and one and a half bathrooms. I also found a babysitter for Zohra who took care of her in her home, which she really enjoyed. Zohra hated coming home, and would kick and scream every time I would go to pick her up from the babysitter. I actually had to bribe her with candy to come home with me.

She was growing up fast, and every day she would learn something new. She loved playing with her toys and picking up the phone all the time. The first time she started walking, she had my

T-shirt on halfway, walking down the hall with her arms stretched out for balance. I took a picture of her right then and there and kept my camera close by for more candid photos of her antics. I did not want to miss a thing that she did while she was growing up in our little apartment.

Financially, we were able to make ends meet, and I still made time to be together with my family. Unfortunately, though, my anxiety started to creep up again. I was always afraid of my child getting hurt without me around. I became anxious at work and also at the community college, where I was taking English classes again. Sometimes, I would get so nervous I would have to leave in the middle of the class and go home.

Dean joined a club nearby and started dancing again. One night, I really wanted him home with me. As a joke, I hid his keys behind my back so he could not leave. Dean threw me on the couch in the living room, pulled my hair and grabbed the keys from my hands. He told me, "Never do that again!" and stormed out the door. When he got angry, his eyes would bulge, and he would become uncontrollable. This was the first time he got physical with me. I felt so hurt and belittled by what he did; I put Zohra to bed and then cried myself to sleep.

~~~

As things became tenser for him, Dean became more abusive toward Zohra and me – emotionally and physically. He criticized me all the time about everything. He accused me of not being sexy enough, having small breasts, having bad breath, not being brave enough, being too skinny, too dark, a clean freak. He accused me of spoiling the baby, spending too much time with my family, and he criticized my family for not respecting him enough. He blamed Zohra and me for being in his way and for being tied down. He kept saying, "I never wanted to get married. It was all those stupid Afghans that kept pushing me into it."

He constantly complained of how much he hated his life. He hated everybody. No one was smart enough or good enough at work or anywhere else, and he even complained about his family back home. Nothing was right.

I tried to console him, telling him that things would eventually get better, to be patient and enjoy life for what we had; to be thankful for our good health, our child, our freedom and now we have a house. "We have to appreciate those things," I said. "Where we came from and the life that we had back home is now the war zone of the world." He wouldn't hear any of it.

When the price of housing in Northern Virginia went up, and the area became more and more crowded, we decided to move to Richmond, Virginia. We rented another apartment for a lot less money and transferred to new jobs there. Eventually we purchased a home, and our mortgage payment was less than our rent in Northern Virginia.

While we were living in the apartment in Richmond, I started getting sick. It started off as a minor thing, but I kept getting sicker and sicker. I could feel the stress catching up to me. My legs started hurting, my ankles swelled up and my knees became painful. I could not walk up the stairs. I ended up crawling, and could not even carry my child up to her room. I had a dry cough, and could not catch my breath. I saw different doctors; they all had something to say other then what was really wrong with me. I spent months not knowing what was going on with my body. I was slowing down and becoming crippled. I still carried out my daily chores and went to work, never feeling good at all.

Finally, my primary doctor referred me to a specialist. The second that he looked at my nodules around my ankles, he was shocked. He said, "I've never seen anything like this before," and went to get another doctor to come to see me. They did a biopsy on the little nodules, and then the doctor ordered a chest X-ray. It showed little bubbles all over my lungs. They both agreed it was sarcoidosis, not on my legs but in my lungs. The doctor told me that sarcoidosis was a very rare, severe immune disorder that can kill you quickly. Sarcoidosis can affect any one at any age or race, and it is over 4% fatal. The cause is unknown and anyone can get it. I went through extensive treatment, and was put on high doses of steroids (Prednisone). It affected me physically and emotionally. I became very depressed and my face became puffy. Also, I grew facial hair from the steroids. I kept begging the doctor to put me on an anti-depressant. The doctor kept telling me, "It's OK to be a little depressed. You will get better."

My anxiety level was always high, but this time it was severe. I began to panic, I was unable to sleep at night, and my voice was choking up every time I opened my mouth. I was crying day and night. I was afraid I would die and my little girl would be left without a mom. I couldn't continue working at the bank anymore, where I had been for a couple years. I began to feel anxious handling money and dealing with customers.

Then I started a new job, working at a rehabilitation hospital. I felt better doing this type of work instead of working at the bank. Within a year, my depression slowly went away. The bubbles in my lungs were disappearing, my legs were not swollen and painful anymore, and I didn't die. That had been my worst fear – dying – and through the grace of God, it did not happen. The doctor told me that I could be only in remission, since there was no cure for this disease. I had to do follow-ups and be very careful. But I was so relieved.

~~~

I went on to enroll in a practical nursing program nearby. I wanted to get back into nursing, since I couldn't pass the CGFNS exam (though I had taken it twice by this point). I truly felt like this was going to help me, so I went to school every day and worked on weekends. But I still found time to spend with Zohra. She was about five years old now. She was so good; she would wait until I finished my homework, and then I would spend the rest of the evening with her, swinging on the swing set. She would say, "Higher, push higher, Mommy!" Or we would ride bikes around the block together and to the little high school park.

In the classroom, I sat all the way in the back. There were about twenty-five students in the classroom, all ages. The instructor was a middle-aged woman who was very nice and taught the first half of the program. She gave us assignments and was serious about homework. I, of course, did all my homework. That was no problem at all. The problem came when she told us, "You'll have to do presentations."

I remember that day clearly. I waited until everyone left. I went to my teacher and said, "There's no way I can do the presentations." My instructor did not understand what I was talking about. I had to make myself clear, and tell her that I had a fear of speaking in front of the class. She said, "You must do it in order to get over it. You'll be OK." I was shaking my head, thinking, *no, you don't understand how hard it is.*

As soon as I got home, I made an appointment with a psychologist. I met with her and told her my story. The psychologist didn't have that magic pill to make my fears disappear, so she referred me to a psychiatrist. But it was not soon enough – I needed something for Wednesday and it was Monday. So the psychiatrist prescribed Inderal for me, which seems to work for performance anxiety. I was so happy that I finally got something to help me. Wednesday came, and it was my turn to go up in front of the class and make my presentation. I made a presentation about AIDS. I started out awkwardly, and my classmates were looking at me strangely. But my instructor kept telling me I was doing just fine. I was glad when it was over, and I thanked God for not letting me pass out. My chest did not hurt the way it did before when I was a child in school.

I kept up with my schoolwork, class participation and presentations (I was able to avoid some of them). I wasn't the student that participated the most in my class, but I was better. I worked hard to get comfortable with public speaking. I continued my counseling sessions, attended a phobia support group, and (believe it or not) I even joined Toastmasters of America. I was glad there was such a thing, and that I was not alone. There are so many people who suffer from this phobia. I even managed to help someone with agoraphobia by going to the grocery store with him a few times.

After two years, I graduated. I should have been happy, but I could not help getting more anxious, because now I had to go out into the real world and practice what I learned. I cried and cried, and nothing could calm me. I took the LPN state board exam and I passed, of course.

The rehabilitation hospital I had been working at as a nurse's assistant hired me immediately as an LPN. I was a great nurse, and I worked hard all day. The times I was most uncomfortable were when I had to report to the oncoming shift, or if I needed to talk to the doctors. These things were difficult for me, but they were getting easier. I even took the CGFNS for RN, thinking that the third time is a charm, and I passed. My dream came true and couldn't believe it! It took me a while to realize it was true. Then I had to take the RN state board exam, and passed that, too. I started working as an RN at the rehab hospital right away.

I was doing great as an RN, and definitely making more money than I was as a CNA or LPN. I had to learn to make decisions and judgments concerning patient care, but I had the support of many good and experienced nurses that worked there. They were very helpful and caring, and I became more comfortable over time.

~ Nineteen ~

Another Goal

Now that I had reached my long-term goal of becoming an RN, a year passed and another goal started floating around in my busy head. I wanted to have another baby, but Dean did not. He said, "If you do have another baby, you will be solely responsible for it, and I won't have anything to do with it." I didn't care.

When I got pregnant, I was so excited, and so was Zohra, because she wanted a baby brother or sister. She had told me, "Mom I want a baby for my birthday, and Christmas." Unfortunately, when I was seven weeks pregnant, I miscarried. That was a big blow to me, and to Zohra as well. Then I became pregnant the second time, and this lasted for ten weeks and lost the baby again. This time I was actually devastated. I started sobbing at the doctor's office. I felt so alone for wanting to have a baby and not having much luck with it. I thought maybe it was God's will, since Dean didn't want me to have another baby. Dean told me that he was not going to try again. He informed me that he did not want to put me through this again or himself.

We left things alone for a while. One day when I went to the kitchen in the morning, I felt dizzy and light headed, and had to stop for a second. Then, the same thing happened the next day. I felt a sense of joy for a second, thinking this might be it. I went and bought a home pregnancy test. I couldn't believe it when the test turned out positive; I was so excited. Suddenly I remembered that I had to tell Dean. I was afraid that he was going to make me have an abortion, and I would not allow that to happen. Then I thought, if I keep it from him until I am twelve weeks pregnant, it will be too late to have an abortion. I kept playing with this idea and all of a sudden, it made sense; I was not going to tell him right away.

Deep down I was so happy and felt wonderful. I couldn't wait to tell the whole world, but not just yet. I finally told Dean when I was twelve weeks pregnant, and the reason why I didn't tell him. He didn't say anything at first, and then he said he would not have made me have an abortion.

"I am not that kind of a person. Nevertheless," he reminded me, "as I said before, you are totally responsible for the total care of the baby, and do not ask me to help you in any way." I expected that from him. I was relieved that I could finally tell everyone about my pregnancy, and I made an appointment with the doctor. Dean and Zohra went with me to the doctor the day of my sonogram, and the doctor told us it was boy. Even Dean was happy, and we went out to lunch to celebrate. This time, my pregnancy was uneventful, without much morning sickness, and I enjoyed my pregnancy very much this time.

~~~

I continued to work full time and my stress level was less than before. I learned to focus on some daily stress relief and plan for the new baby boy. I also had an amniocentesis, since I was over thirty-five years of age. That was the most nerve-wracking point of the pregnancy for me – the procedure itself. The results came in when I was sitting in a report room at work. My heart jumped when I heard the woman over the phone, telling me that she had my amniocentesis results. I was silent, my heart pounding, thinking, Oh God, please let it be OK. Dean kept telling me if the baby had some kind of abnormality like Down's syndrome or anything even remotely similar to that, he would want me to terminate the pregnancy.

"Everything is OK. And it's confirmed that it's a boy," the woman on the other end of the phone said. I was shaking and felt a big sense of relief.

I whispered, "Thank you," and hung up the phone. I just sat in the chair – it took me a while to get the strength back in my legs. When I looked up, everyone in the room was staring at me, wondering what had just happened. I apologized for disturbing the shift report, and they went on working.

I couldn't wait to tell Dean the good news. I knew I didn't have any reason to be afraid anymore. Everything was going really well. I went to my appointments by myself. Dean didn't join me anymore. Before I could even wrap my mind around just "being" pregnant, the day came when I went in to labor. Dean went with me to the doctor that morning. The doctor, though, told me I had a couple more days to go. So, I went home, laboring all day. Zohra, who was eight at the time, was at home with me. I kept facing the sofa with my contractions so Zohra would not see me in pain and get worried.

I couldn't tolerate the pain anymore by around 5 pm. I called Dean to come and take me to the hospital. Dean told me, "It's not time yet, since the doctor told you this morning you had a couple more days." I called him the second time and his manager picked up the phone. I said, "I am in labor. Send him home!" She said she would send him home right away. He got home, fussing at me that I was just wasting his time. In the car going to the hospital, I was rolling from side to side in pain. The very second that I got into the labor room and onto the table, my water broke and I was dilated five centimeters (in labor terms, that's halfway to delivering the baby). At around 9 pm, I delivered a beautiful little boy. I fell in love with him at first sight. We named him Jay and I remember his cries were loud and vital, and I knew I had a healthy baby.

Zaman and Ria came to see the new baby and me. After we went home, Ria's mom, who immigrated three years earlier, came for a week to help me with Jay. I was happy that she was able to help me, as I was exhausted. Dean took a week of paternity leave, but instead of helping me with the baby, he started a big project of his own. He started planting new grass in the front yard and worked on that all day. He actually expected my brother Zaman to help him. He was upset when Zaman paid more attention to the new baby and me than to his lawn.

After Zaman and Ria left, I was so busy with the baby, that I did not even have time to fix myself food. I found myself starving, and I wished someone would get me something to eat. My new baby was very colicky, and he cried all day. I carried him around the house all day and tried to comfort him without success.

When Dean came home in the evening, I would give him Jay at the door and leave for a quick walk to get my frustration out. As soon as I came home (no exaggeration here, but almost every single day), Dean would make me take Jay to the doctor. He kept saying, "Something is not right with him, and he needs to be seen by his doctor." I, of course, would then take him to the pediatrician.

The doctor would see Jay again in his office and reassure me that, "Everything is OK. He is just colicky," and I would come home with the same answer that I gave Dean the night before.

"He shouldn't cry so much. Or, he's hungry and you don't know how to feed him," Dean kept saying.

Jay was nursing and supplementing, and he ate quite well, actually. But he screamed and cried for six weeks. He just couldn't tolerate my milk. As soon as I stopped nursing him, he stopped crying. And now I was crying, because I thought the nursing was going better than it did with Zohra. I had been very impressed with the one thing I "thought" I was doing right.

Jay grew like a weed and got better with his daily activities. Zohra had fun with him, and she was a big help. Some days, though, she would wake him up from his nap when I wasn't looking (she told me later on that she got bored or missed him and wanted to play). His crib was in her room, and every time he woke up and cried, she was there to comfort him. Of course, when this happened, she would be very tired the next day (Dean wouldn't let me use the spare room as a nursery, because that was where he had his office).

I started going back to work part-time after twelve weeks. I enjoyed going to work, and we needed the money. Life actually then seemed to plateau for the next couple of years into some sort of a routine.

It then became more difficult again. As my son got to be a couple of years old, I had to take him to a day care. He didn't like to be dropped off at the day care. The workers would have to peel him off me every time I dropped him off, and it broke my heart. I kept him during the day and worked in the evenings, so he stayed at the day care about three to four hours at a time. He hated it. The older he got the worse it got.

One day when he was three years old, he walked out to the parking lot and would not go back in. He told the supervisor, "I don't want to be here!" I received a phone call from the frantic supervisor, telling me to come and pick him up. I was informed,

"If he gets hurt or walks away, we are not going to be responsible for him." Of course, I picked him up right away and never took him back to that place again. I ended up working nights and keeping him during the day. He was happy then.

~ Twenty ~

An Unhappy Marriage

Things were getting progressively worse with Dean and me. He was getting physically abusive. Once, when Jay was only two years old, he was screaming and wanted his mommy. He was stretching his arms towards me, and Dean pushed him down into his crib to try to make him go to sleep.

I moved toward the crib to give Dean a break, and get him out of the way before he injured Jay. I picked up Jay to comfort him. Before I knew it, Dean was pulling me by the hair. He threw me on Zohra's bed, and started punching me while I was holding Jay. Zohra heard all the commotion and came into the room. She was horrified.

Dean left the house, slamming the door as he left. I couldn't help feeling sorry for myself, and I started to cry, all while my little children were clinging to me. Zohra made me tea and toast, hoping it would make her mother feel better. When Dean came back hours later, he acted as if nothing happened, and he expected me to apologize for butting in. I just went on with my usual chores and hated him for a few days, and then I continued to act as if nothing had happened either; that is how our disagreements went. I had to keep the kids quiet by giving in to their demands, so he wouldn't get upset and hurt them or me. If I didn't, he would scold me for spoiling my children and ruining his life.

He continued to go out ballroom dancing once or twice a week. I stayed home alone with my children on the nights I was off work. If I dared to complain, he would tell me, "It's your problem – you're the one who wanted to have children."

I worked nights because Jay couldn't tolerate daycare. Dean had never liked taking care of the kids, so he would leave Jay with Zohra (now ten years old) to babysit. The nights he went dancing, I didn't know where he took the children. He would say it was inconvenient for him to arrange for babysitting, and he usually took them to people he knew, so he didn't have to pay.

Dean was especially hard on Zohra, since she was a girl. She was supposed to be proper and polite and help me with the household chores. He made her wash the dishes and wipe down the dining table. He made her cry at the dinner table every night, making her finish her food, no matter if she was full or not. She didn't like onions, as they made her sick to her stomach. Unfortunately, most Afghan food has onions in it, and I made it that way to make him happy. Dean wouldn't let her pick out the onions and he made her eat them. She would cry, and end up throwing up in the bathroom afterwards. It made me anxious and stressed, and I hated him for that, but I couldn't defend her or myself.

He taught her The Holy Quran, and made her recite it in front of the family members and friends just to show off what a "good little girl" he had. He made her go to sleep at 8 pm every night, no matter where we were or what day of the week it was. She was not an early sleeper. When we were at Ria's house, she liked the attention of her mom and aunt trying to put her to sleep. As soon as we left, thinking that she was asleep, Zohra would open her eyes and call us to come back to her. As a result, I had to spend one or two hours a night trying to put Zohra to sleep. If I didn't, Dean would get mad at us, and the whole night would be ruined.

~~~

In 1995, my brother Amir immigrated with his wife and children to Waynesboro, Virginia. Zaman sponsored him, and they found a house near his. I wanted to visit my brothers on the weekends I was off work, and Dean wasn't happy about that, either. A couple of years later, he told me if I wanted us to move closer to where my brothers were living (about 100 miles away), that would be OK. His only condition was that he would not have any responsibility for the children or me. He said I would have to ask my brothers if I needed help. I was fine with that, for I knew that I wasn't really losing or gaining much by staying anyhow (this was a few weeks after he punched me).

In October 1998, we moved to Waynesboro, Virginia, to be near my brothers. I got a good job at Augusta Medical Center, in the labor and delivery unit, which was my specialty. Dean was transferred to a DMV to Waynesboro. The kids and I moved a couple weeks before Dean, and stayed with my brothers. Dean said he wanted to stay back and take care of the house details, even though my brothers and sisters-in-law and I had already packed all the boxes and painted the house.

I really didn't want Dean to move with us, but I was not brave enough to tell him. I hated his guts, but I still couldn't leave him. That was not our custom. In our culture, no matter how unhappy I was, I was supposed to pretend to everyone that things were OK. I dreamed he would somehow just disappear. I wanted to pack up my kids and myself, rent a truck and go far away where he couldn't find us.

Once again, I was trying to start a new job and enroll Zohra in her new school, all while taking care of Jay and trying to look for an apartment. There wasn't much available in the area to rent. My brother Amir talked to his landlord, and managed to persuade him into renting an apartment to us. I was happy to be living close to my brothers, and to be able to see them more often. Now I had something to do while Dean spent his time going out dancing.

Dean was very rude to the kids and me, and never let up on the pressure that he applied. He kept complaining about my brothers and about the area, his job, the people he worked with, and everything else. The apartment was very small, with two bedrooms. The kids shared one room, and Zohra never had any peace.

I constantly begged him to move into a house. He didn't want to buy an expensive house (to him anything above $100,000 was expensive – and this was in the year 2000). He wanted to find an old house for next to nothing, and maybe fix it up, as long as it was going to be cheap. Finally, after a year of searching, we found a nice, big house for a price that we could afford. It had three levels, four bedrooms with walk-in closets, a Jacuzzi tub, a pool table, fireplace, and a big patio and back yard. I was so excited about decorating the new house and choosing curtains. I felt like we could start over and things would be better between Dean and me after we were settled. We actually were happier for a while, as we had a lot of family and friends visit us in our new home and enjoyed their company.

Jay still didn't like any of the daycares, so I went back to working the nightshift in order to take care of Jay during the day. Again, Dean was not happy about me working at night. He didn't want to take care of the kids or find a babysitter for them when he went dancing. "You are making things very inconvenient for me again," he said.

Déjà vu was rearing its ugly head.

Again, Dean's dancing took priority, and he left the kids at various friends' houses when he went out. He punished Jay if he didn't listen to him or if he didn't go to sleep on time. Months later, I found out that Dean would take Jay down into the dark basement. Zohra told me she would hear Jay crying and screaming from the basement (she unfortunately had to hear it through the laundry chute that was in her room). Dean would tell her not to tell me about this nightly terror, and since she was so afraid, Zohra never did. It broke my heart that she had to suffer as a result.

During the day, Dean made Zohra babysit most of the time. She was only eleven then. She began to not want to hang out with us much and just wanted to be with her friends. I didn't blame her, although at the time, I still did not fully understand the extent as to "why" she felt this way.

One time, we were taking Jay to the park, and she didn't want to go. Her dad was mad at her for refusing to go. He went into her room and punched her in the forehead while I was getting Jay ready. Before we left, I asked, "Where is Zohra?" Dean just said, "Zohra is not going."

When we came back, I saw her swollen face. It turned out that she had a big cut and bruise and was bleeding above her eyebrow. I was so distraught and upset; I felt like such a loser. I should have punched him or tried to, at the very least, but I wasn't brave enough. It killed me to see her go through that. I felt so helpless and dominated.

Zohra had to cover her forehead and eye with her hair for the next few days to hide the bruise. She became very quiet and depressed. She never wanted to go anywhere. She wanted me to paint her room very dark blue, which I did. She had her blinds down at all times. She binged with her eating.

One night, Zohra had just come home from being out with her friends. She was fourteen years old. She told us that she wasn't hungry. Her dad got mad at her for not eating dinner with us, and yelled and screamed at her. She just went to her room and stayed there.

Later on, at about 2 am, she came into our bedroom, stumbling and crying. I jumped out of bed to see what was going on. Zohra was dizzy and throwing up.

She kept saying, "I just wanted to kill myself."

I took her to the bathroom, and asked her, "What did you take?" Zohra had taken a handful of Tylenol and a bottle of Robitussin. Dean was still sleeping. I told him what had happened.

He turned onto his side and said, "Apparently it did not work. Let me go tell her how to kill herself." I started crying and told him that I was going to take her to the emergency room.

"She's fine. Let her sleep it off," he said. Then he took his pillow and went to the guest room to sleep. Apparently, Zohra and I were bothering him.

While I was driving Zohra to the hospital, I was shaking the whole time. I couldn't believe things had gotten so bad for her. I felt so alone dealing with this situation, but I tried to be strong for her.

I stayed with her in the hospital until morning. Fortunately, her blood levels were normal but the doctor wanted to hospitalize her and monitor for the suicide attempt. I told him that I was a nurse and would watch her and make sure that she was safe. We came home at 6 am, emotionally drained and scared.

I couldn't believe that I had let things get so out of control just to save our marriage – a marriage that was never a two-way street. I stayed home for the next few days, just taking care of my daughter, and I made sure she got counseling. That is when I realized that I did not want my children to hurt anymore. I felt that by allowing this to continue one moment longer, I was the one hurting them. They were my children and my responsibility. And it was their right to feel safe. I could deal with myself getting hurt, but not my children. I had tried to tough it out all those years, but I was not going to take the chance of losing my daughter because of my husband. It was not worth it. That was the last straw. I became brave. I became outraged. I loved my kids too much to let him hurt them again.

A few weeks before this incident, my anxiety level had peaked, and I had gone to the doctor. I started taking an incredible anti-anxiety medicine called Paxil. It made a world of difference in my life. All of a sudden, I felt confident. I wasn't that scared little Afghan girl anymore. I wouldn't take Dean's shit anymore. I woke up and became a new person that wasn't caged or stuck in a hole. I did not want to be in that hole anymore, nor would I allow it for my children.

The day after Zohra's suicide attempt, I told Dean that I was going to leave him. He needed to feel committed to his kids and not to consider them "obstacles" as he called them all the time. He always said that he didn't want to be tied down by a wife and kids. He wanted to do his own thing.

He did not think I would leave him. At first I didn't mention the word, "divorce." I guess I couldn't bring myself to say it.

"Why don't you ever tell me you love me?" I asked him.

"Do you want me to lie?" he said.

So I told him that since we were not happy together, and he wanted to be left alone and didn't want to have anything to do with the children, it was best for us to go our own separate ways. I didn't want my children to get hurt anymore. He said there was nothing wrong with our marriage.

He told me, "You leave the house, because I'm not going." So, I decided to try counseling or mediation first, hoping it would help us work things out. Unfortunately, it didn't. And I ended up paying the bills for that, too (he said it was my idea, so it was my responsibility. Until I found a new place to move into, I had to live in the same house with him for six months while we were separated. I had packed my stuff and left all the boxes in my room. Later, I realized that whenever I went to work at night, he was coming in to my room and stealing things out of my boxes.

I just didn't realize he would go that far – to steal my photo albums and personal items that friends and family had given me. I found out only after I moved out. When I confronted him, he denied it, of course.

~~~

I bought a little house in the "Tree Streets" area of Waynesboro. It took awhile to finish the details, and in the meantime, he kept harassing me. "Take your kids and go to a hotel," he would say, "so I can get on with my life."

Finally, in June 2001, the day of the move came. My brothers and their families helped. Dean stayed home that day and fought over every little detail he could fight about. I ended up only taking my bedroom set and my kids' sets that I had paid for.

I was so excited to move in to my own home. I painted every room a different color – anything my kids and I liked. I enjoyed being my own boss. I didn't have to get permission from anyone for anything anymore.

After closing on the house, my children and I spent the first night on the sofa bed that was left downstairs by the previous owner. We all slept together. I felt free, and I felt like there was a mountain lifted off my shoulders. I didn't feel like a prisoner anymore. Zohra and Jay were so happy. They just cuddled up with me and we all slept like babies. Jay called it "the princess bed."

Zohra started cleaning her room and organizing her clothes. She was a big help to me. Her sunny room faced our beautiful backyard garden. She wanted her room painted bright yellow, so that's what we did. What a change from that dark, depressive blue. Yellow was the perfect color to represent the way our lives had completely changed and brightened.

Jay had a bunk bed that was given to us by one of my friends. They even brought the bed to my house on a rainy day. Rica's husband Ryan was soaking wet. I couldn't believe someone could be so kind and sensitive. Do people like that still exist? I cried when I saw this couple with such kindness in their hearts. I was very appreciative.

I settled into my new little house, and decorated every room. I took care of my lawn – I mowed, and planted new grass, trees, flowers, and vegetables. I was very proud of myself. We got a kitten from the SPCA and a little poodle from a friend.

The second year that I was in my new home, I was very content. I worked nights and stayed home during the day with my kids. The nights I worked, Jay spent with his dad or my brothers, since someone had to drive him to school the next morning. Jay was five years old, and just like any other little boy, he wanted things and he wanted them now! Both Zohra and I had to calm him down and work with him.

Dean hardly ever kept his appointments whenever we arranged for him to drop off or pick up Jay. Some days, he wouldn't even show up at all. Then I would have to find someone else to take Jay to the sitter before going to work. As a result, I would be late for work. Jay would get upset, and we would both feel stressed. But later on, Jay got used to his father's inconsistencies. He would say, "He might not show up, Mom," or "He will be here," or "He is late as usual."

Zohra was now fourteen years old. Her dad kept pushing her to come to his house to visit, but she did not want to spend time with him. She kept saying no, and she told me she was not going to put up with his demands.

A few months after moving into my new house, Dean visited and brought a bunch of flowers. He asked me to come back.

"It's time for us to get back together, since this was a lesson for everybody, especially for you," he said.

"Yes," I said, "this was actually a very good lesson for me, and I am going to stick with it." I threw his flowers in the trash and laughed as I came back inside. Nothing was going to make me go back to him. I finalized the divorce papers with my lawyer and paid for it all, with no help from him.

We had to go to court twice – the first time was for the divorce. I had never been in court before, and I started out shaky and nervous. The second time was because Dean kicked my car. It happened one evening when I was dropping off Jay. I was sitting in the car, and Dean came after me wanting to argue about some nonsense issue. He was screaming and yelling with Jay standing there. I didn't want to talk to him, so I started to roll up the window. Then he kicked my car, making a big dent.

I was very scared, and didn't know what to do. I called a new friend I had met, named Tim, who immediately came and comforted me. He went with me to the police station and helped me file a complaint. The judge ruled in my favor, and Dean had to pay damages to fix my car.

Tim accompanied me to court and stayed with me every time I dropped off Jay. He was a big shoulder for me to lean on in these times of distress. I felt I had a bodyguard. I felt safe.

~ Twenty-One ~

Tim

I had actually met Tim online in May of 2002, after moving into my new home. The nights I didn't have to work, I could not sleep at all. I stayed on the computer after the kids went to sleep, mostly playing games.

One night, I was browsing through Internet dating sites, and checking out profiles, even though I promised myself I would never get involved with anyone again (unless God was going to send an angel from out of the sky to me). Some of the profiles were very weird. But all of a sudden, someone appeared on the screen I never expected to see. He lived in the little town of Waynesboro – the very same town that I lived in. He was wearing an olive-colored shirt that complimented his green-blue eyes. And he had a smile that could melt ice.

In his profile, he said that he was thirty-seven years old, 5'10", straight, a nonsmoker and a Christian. He was a professional who enjoyed hiking, jogging, swimming, biking and walking, as well as pubs, board games, fine dining, music, traveling, gourmet cooking, concerts, family, and so much more. His profile stated, "I love life and all it has to offer. I'm a pragmatist in all things except love, where I am a hopeless romantic." He said his dream mate would be someone able to be honest and true about who they are, and who can express how they feel. "You must love children, as mine are part of who I am," he wrote. It all sounded very impressive.

For some strange reason, I decided to step out on a limb and send him a little hello, mentioning that I lived in the same town. I didn't think much about it. He wrote me the next day and wanted to hear more about me, so I wrote more about myself. He wrote again and said, "You sound like a very interesting person, and we already have something in common." He said that by training, he was an X-ray tech, and a Hospital Corpsman in the Navy in the late 80s. As of six months ago, he had taken the job of Finance Manager for the radiology department at the University Hospital, where he had previously been the Diagnostic Imaging Manager. He loved his job; it allowed him to use his head, and not destroy his body (the medical field is a tough one). His job was Monday-Friday, with weekends and holidays off, which was great for his girls and himself. He asked me for my e-mail so that we could communicate more directly.

He also wrote poems.

His first poem that he sent me was about trust:

Trust

How can I show thee what my heart does not hide?...
Questionably you look to my soul and wonder,
"When?"
When will it turn on me...those words said so oft before?
Always in vain and deceit spoken, never truly known what they mean
A litany of lies upon lies, years upon years, time after time
How can you trust in this one, when you cannot even trust in yourself?
A fear caused by all that has been etched upon your heart so true

This fateful word, so complex, yet too simple to let alone

We search in earnest for it, prizing it highest upon our list

But cringing in fear of it when we think it's finally discovered

Running in terror because of the similarity in all that we have seen

An elusive creature with many evil twins running amok

Inflicting pain and heartache in the wake of their path

But, in the blackest of all the midnights, was FINALLY see

Understood, we realize that it is out there, honest and real

Not a myth after all, nor a fairy tale spun from yarn

But a warmth to our heart and a beacon to our soul

In the darkest of these times, we finally see it so true

It guides us finally home to where we belong

I have given my hand to you.... Given you my faith and soul

Only able to offer you who I am and nothing more

Spending every moment hoping only to ease the pain in your heart

Wanting to show you the beauty that God has given to my soul

Taking day by day, never to waiver from whom I really am

I proclaim my love for Him and for you long through the day

In addition, celebrate in all of the Trust and Love that I have in you

~ T. Ulrich

I read his poem and showed it to some of my friends at work. I was amazed at how talented he was and how he felt. It was somewhat unreal for me. I had never met a man with that much sensitivity and ability to show emotions. I wrote back and said I liked the poem.

The next day he wrote, "I'm glad that you enjoyed the poem. I take it that this is your weekend to work, since I got the e-mail from your work address. I used to work weekends myself, so I know how it is. As for my girls, Nichole is twelve and Marin will turn eleven in July. They are my Godsend and have made me the man I am. What kind of food you like? Do you like to go out, and if so, is it tough for you to find a babysitter, or is that taken care of, having a 14-year-old? What are some of your favorite things to do? In addition, do you like to travel?"

And then, he sent me another poem:

Our Forever More

Standing on the cliffs, as we have always forced to do
We can appreciate all of life's gifts, it's highs and its lows
Every nuance of the human soul that has been etched in to our brain
Knowing that EVERY person has a unique gift of which to give
And that even the most misguided are just trying to find their way
And even though they hurt us, they are full of pain none the same
A poison so deadly that it eats them away from the inside
We resolve to love them anyway, but not in the way that they demand
And deal with them by not only in compassion
But from a vantage of distance and of strength

Many times having been tripped, but never having fallen, we carry on
Determined to take ourselves to a higher plane of being
and to live the life that we have dreamed of for so long
We dust ourselves off, and plan how to do what we must
To grant ourselves the gift of friendship and life eternal
We continue our travels for this place we must find
And believe that we have come to know is true

For beyond all of the twists, turns and mysteries of our time
Lies a place unlike any ever known or ever seen
An ethereal-like land of unparalleled beauty and of light

Home to a warmth, peace and of eternal joy
For in this real-life mystical utopia exists a different breed of soul
Those who have sacrificed for all that they truly love
And have refused to give an ounce, not a single speck
To those who would try to take their life, and very breath
My dearest Love…you and I, though separate and currently apart
Are on this path of love and light, and travel together as one
We have and will continue to always do what is just and right
To see us into the morn of not only tomorrow and the day
But to walk together into the land of love ever eternal
That place we ultimately desire… Our Forever More
~ T. Ulrich

I was very interested in reading his poems and letters. My friends at work were amazed by him and wanted me to keep in touch with him. They kept telling me, "He sounds like a very nice person." We started instant messaging each other around 9 pm every night, after we both put our kids to bed. One night, Zohra was helping me type, since I was not that adept with typing or short cuts. He sent me more of his poems. I responded and said how beautiful they were, and how I knew they were deep, and from the heart.

This went on for a while. Every night I looked forward to talking to him on the phone or on instant messenger. One night, I made another leap and I asked him about his marital status. He said that he had been divorced for over two years, and separated for two years before that. I told him I was separated, but not divorced yet – that it was in the process. He told me that he knew how it felt."Eventually it is like a great weight off the shoulders, and then you go on," he said. I told him about my children and how they were the love of my life, and how much strength and power they had given me to go through what

I had been through all these years. I told him about my background, education, family and so on. I shared as much as I dared.

I remember in one of his first letters, he wanted me to send my picture but then suddenly reversed himself, saying "I don't need a picture, as I can tell you are a beautiful person inside and out just from talking to you." Things were getting deep between us. We had discussed getting together before now, but I wasn't ready to meet him in person just yet.

After a couple of months, we decided to meet. It was at a small restaurant in town, called Mossy Creek. I was nervous, yet excited. It was at 6 pm, just an hour before I had to go to work. I wore casual clothes, and my dark brown hair hung over my shoulders. As I walked into the restaurant, he approached me and greeted me with a bouquet of flowers. He pulled out the chair for me to sit down, and he sat across the table from me. He looked exactly like his picture (which I hear never happens). His blue eyes were bright and piercing, but not intimidating. Later I found out the color of his eyes changed in different situations. It was like his mood ring.

We ordered iced tea, and he drank a lot of it as we talked. Tim did most of the talking. He didn't seem nervous at all, other than spilling tea on his necktie a few times. I was kind of shy and quiet. I answered some of his questions. He walked me to my car, opened the car door for me, and gave me a hug before I got in. Everything about our meeting impressed me, but the time went by so fast.

As soon as I got to work, I told my friends about the date. They were teasing me, saying, "You have a glow." I told them that Tim had asked me to go hiking the following week, and I agreed. My friends decided it would be fun to scare me.

"He might be a criminal or a psychopath," they said. "You shouldn't go. He might get you drunk, kill you and throw you down a cliff."

That Saturday, Tim showed up with a picnic basket and sparkling grape juice, seafood salad, cranberry salad and sandwiches. I was nervous at first, thinking the sparkling grape juice was wine, but I was relieved after I read the label.

I was not afraid of him. Something about him put me at ease the first time we met. The hike was short – we didn't go far. We walked up to Humpback Rock in the Blue Ridge Mountains. As we were coming back down, he kissed me for the first time. It was nothing like I had experienced before. It made me feel warm, and I blushed.

He immediately said, "I apologize for making you uncomfortable." I told him, "It's OK." I really kind of liked it, but didn't want to make too much out of it. Of course, since this was so new (though we had been talking for two months now), I didn't tell him where I lived. So, we met at the grocery store parking lot, and that's where we said goodbye that day.

It turned out that Tim actually lived less than two miles from my house. Our children went to the same schools. We shopped at the same grocery store, and even went to the same library. Everyone in our little town knew each other; it was odd that we had never run into each other before. God has a dry sense of humor when it comes down to it, but he knows His timing (well, it is His creation, after all).

~~~

After dating for a while, we introduced our kids to each other. His kids were friendly and got along with Zohra and Jay. My kids, on the other hand, had their good days and their bad. Jay had a good time at Tim's house, being with Marin and Nichole. He actually got to the point that sometimes he didn't want to come home. He said, "They have more snacks and cookies than we do." It took Zohra a long time to warm up to Tim, however. Tim was patient, and gave her plenty of time and space. Some days, 6-year-old Jay would become irrational and defiant, throwing things and screaming – especially after coming home from visiting his dad. On those days, Tim would sit in Jay's room for hours, talking with him until he settled down. He was the only one who could calm him down. Due to Tim's quiet patience and firm, but extremely loving way of dealing with these outbursts, they occurred less and less as time went by.

We had been dating for six or seven months, and Tim continued to be kind and gentle, and respected my children and me. He comforted me during my stressful times, and we talked about everything and anything. I felt like I had known him all my life. Even though we came from different cultures, we had so much in common. We were constantly at each other's houses with our kids. Our kids even went to the same Taekwondo martial arts center. We loved taking pictures of our kids. He was so involved in his kid's activities – as much as I was. And I was very impressed with how he dealt with them – always in such calm manner, and always giving them support. He washed and ironed his girls' clothes. He brushed their hair, made ponytails, and even braided their hair. He helped them with their school projects. He cooked and cleaned for them. He took them to the doctors and emergency room when they were sick. He took care of his kids the same way I did mine, and it made me happy.

I thought, this is so unreal. I was waiting for the other shoe to drop. I didn't know a man could have such profound abilities with kids and other aspects of life in general. He constantly reminded me, "It is all real. I am just myself, nothing more, nothing less."

His mother lived with him to help him with the girls, and she seemed very kind and friendly. We all went to picnics, drive-in movies, recreational parks and restaurants. Zohra didn't join us as much. Well, she was fifteen. She only wanted to hang out with her friends. She still didn't trust him, and had a hard time believing in him. She didn't think a man could be that nice and sensitive. We didn't blame her. After what she had been through, we wanted to give her plenty of time and support.

We were getting extremely close, and so I made a big leap. I felt like it was time for me to hint to my brothers about Tim. I wanted him to meet my brothers, and I don't know what I was thinking.

They immediately said, "You are doing something that is a not acceptable in our culture. First of all, you go off and get a divorce, which is absolutely forbidden in our customs. We think you should just stay single and raise your kids. There is nothing wrong with that." They strongly reminded me that Pari, my oldest sister, did it.

"She raised her six children by herself after her husband was killed during the war. And she did just fine," they said.

In reality, Pari was pregnant with her sixth child when her husband was killed. She lived off of his retirement and suffered tremendously. She lived in a small room in my father's family home with all her six children. I wasn't in Afghanistan at the time, but I can imagine how hard it was on her and her kids physically and emotionally.

"Times have changed, and I do need someone in my life to be with me and care for me and my children," I told my brothers.

"We are here for you and your children. You can't let a stranger come into your life and be part of the family," they said. They were probably thinking back to when Dad married Zewar, and how we became like forgotten stepchildren.

"He can't truly care about your kids. He will treat them badly," they warned. I reassured them that this would not happen.

"You need to give him a chance and get to know him. He is different. He has kids, and he knows how to treat them.

I arranged for a picnic at the park with all my family, and I invited Tim. My brothers did come, but they ignored him the whole time. Tim barbecued hamburgers and hot dogs and served everyone. My sisters-in-law did pay some attention, and offered to help him at times. Tim was acutely aware of the situation, and tried not to let it bother him. But I was upset. I was still hopeful that once they got to know him, they would see how nice he is, and that they would come around.

Two months later, I was at my brother's house and I had a huge argument with them. They were chastising me about my life and about Tim.

They told me, "He is an American and not a Muslim. It is our responsibility to protect you and keep you in line. You are not thinking clearly." They were raised to protect their sisters, and it was their duty to tell me this. Since my parents were deceased, they were responsible for my happiness and my protection. In Afghanistan, that's what brothers do.

"I am not in Afghanistan now," I said. "I am here in America, and I am old enough to make my own decisions." I couldn't believe how brave I had become. I couldn't have talked to them like that a year earlier. Then suddenly, I felt guilty for being rude to my older brothers, and I started sobbing.

I was so upset I couldn't even drive myself home. I called Tim, and Zohra came with him to drive me home. Tim got very upset with my brothers, though somehow he kept his composure. He was in the driveway and my sisters-in-law were at the door. In a voice that was more confident than I had ever heard, he said to them, "If anyone needs to say something about me, tell it to my face. I don't ever want to see Anisa this upset anymore, otherwise you will have to answer to me." I couldn't stop crying. I thought someone had punched me in the gut.

~ Twenty-Two ~

True Love

In September 2002, Tim proposed to me. He told me that he wanted to show me his love, and especially to show my family that he was sincere about our relationship. He had wanted to wait until Christmas to propose, but he didn't want my brothers to think he was trying to change my religious beliefs by tying the proposal to the "Christian" holiday of Christmas.

Of course, I said, "Yes." I couldn't believe what was happening, but I knew it was the right thing to do. This time I would pick who I wanted to marry. I was extremely excited, yet scared at the same time. I felt like I wasn't going to have much support from the family, but that was OK; I had him.

We wanted to wait at least six months before we got married. We were constantly at each other's houses with our kids, taking them to ballgames, picnics and movies, carpooling together, making meals and plans together. Keeping two households was getting expensive, so we decided that Tim should move into my house with his kids. Then we would have only one household to worry about.

We all moved into my little three-bedroom house with the basement. Even though there was not much room in the house, the kids actually got along well. They had so much fun, and were making the most of it. His mom got her own place in town, and she was happy about that. She didn't have to worry about taking care of her grandkids anymore, and she could spend time with her own circle of friends.

Both of us were traditional, so after a while, living together without being married didn't feel right. We decided to get married on June 21, 2003. We only had a few weeks to plan our wedding. The only person helping us was my mother-in-law, who arranged for the flowers and table settings. We made a reservation at the Holiday Inn at the Afton Mountain ski resort, and got a good deal, because it was the off-season.

A friend's sister agreed to do the photography for $250.00. I found beautiful brides maid's dresses for Tim's girls and Zohra, who was the maiden of honor. Tim wanted Jay to be his best man. Jay was only six years old at the time, but he asked a most profound question.

"What does a best man do?"

"Just stand next to me," Tim said.

"OK."

He was so composed and mature standing next to Tim. They both looked so adorable.

The big day came. The night before the wedding, the girls and I did our nails, got facials, and had our teeth whitened. We had a blast. The boys stayed at the hotel. The morning of the wedding, the girls and I went to get our hair done. We had such a good time.

That morning, Tim went to pick up the cake. Just as he was bringing it into the front door of the hotel, the bottom layer fell and splattered on the floor. He was panicked, but somehow he convinced the bakery to make another one in an hour (he told me this part after the wedding. I thought it was funny, but I also felt bad for him).

There were about fifty people at the wedding. It was a beautiful, sunny day, at least at the beginning. It started raining as Tim and I were leaving the hotel, buried with rice thrown at us by our children. The large reception room was bright and happy, and it was a joyful moment for us, surrounded by windows overlooking the Blue Ridge Mountains.

The wedding ceremony took place downstairs, in the small chapel of the Holiday Inn Hotel. My friend's husband married us. The ceremony was about to begin, and none of my family had arrived. I kept checking the door. I was scared that nobody would come. Deep down, I was hoping my brothers would come.

At the last second, my aunt Sofia, her sons and their wives' families arrived. My aunt looked regal as she came in through the door. She has so much grace, that everyone in attendance knew there was royalty present. Then my sister-in-law Ria came. I was so relieved. I was worried she wouldn't come. And then Amir's daughter and son, my niece Dee, and nephew Zia, came too. All of sudden, there were a lot of people there, all in support of our love.

The whole day went so well – everything was beautiful and perfectly organized. The Inn catered the food and it was delicious. Tim's oldest brother and his wife came from Illinois, and his mom, of course, was there. Some of our friends showed up as well. I was heartbroken, though, that my brothers did not come. This was due to the fact that I caused the ultimate offense against their personal beliefs and their take on our culture: I had the nerve to marry someone other than an Afghan man.

Then my nephew Aisal walked in, just as I was getting ready to walk down the aisle. I asked him. "Could you walk me down the aisle?" He was somewhat shocked, and didn't know what to do. This tall, handsome man, a gentle soul, now twenty years old, was just a baby when we all fled to the US as refugees. I could still remember the day I delivered him. Now he was standing by my side, accompanying me on this new journey. Maybe it was fate that brought him to the chapel that morning.

I said, "You don't have to do anything special. Just walk with me." He agreed, with a big smile. I was so proud of him.

The flower girl, about two years old, was the daughter of a friend. She wore a white dress, and looked so pretty. She had a basket of red and white rose petals, and was throwing them as she was walking down the aisle. Then she turned around and suddenly started picking the petals back up and putting them in the basket. It was so cute, and it made everyone laugh.

Zohra, Nichole and Marin all wore aqua-blue long dresses and had their hair up. They looked gorgeous. I wore a cream-colored dress, with spaghetti straps and a long, full skirt, and wore my hair up with cream-colored sequins in it. It was simple but elegant. I had on the diamond stud earrings that Tim had given me the Christmas before. I looked and felt vibrant. Nothing bothered me or could have bothered me that day. I was on cloud nine.

I didn't have anyone to play music, so I played some CDs for the wedding march. The ceremony went off without a hitch, and we ended by lighting an eternity candle (which accompanies us to this day). After we were pronounced husband and wife, we danced with each other. Then Tim danced with the kids and finally with his mom. Then the whole crowd joined in and there was so much love in the air, I felt like we could scoop it up and drink it with a cup.

After the ceremony, Tim and I got the chance to be alone in the chapel for a few minutes. As long as I live, I will never forget that moment; the image is burned into my brain. As we looked at each other, Tim suddenly walked over to the stereo and played one last song. I gasped; it was our song, "Always and Forever," by Heatwave:

> *Everyday, love me your own special way*
> *Melt all my heart away with a smile*
> *Take time to tell me you really care*
> *And we'll share tomorrow together*
> *I'll always love you*

We danced in the chapel for a long time after everyone went up to the reception area. It was magical.

Tim and me on our wedding day.
~~~

We went for a weekend honeymoon – short and sweet. It was a trip to West Virginia, just to get away from it all. Somehow, Tim managed to get me onto a horse for the first and only time in my life. We just spent the time walking, talking and knowing that we both were complete for the very first time in our lives. For the first time ever, I felt no fear.

When we came back and got settled in, it was like we had been together as a family forever. The kids got along really well. Jay loved to be around his new sisters, and they loved to be around him. He was happy that we had a big family now. Zohra was still adjusting, but was getting along better with her new stepfamily.

Unfortunately, it became quite clear that the house was a little small for the six of us. In July 2003, exactly one month after the wedding, we bought a 3500-square-foot brick house. It had five bedrooms, each with private bathrooms and walk in closets. It had a Jacuzzi bath, and two laundry rooms. Zohra and Nichole each had their own bedrooms on the first floor, Marin's was on the main floor and ours and Jay's on the third floor; there were lots of stairs.

We had a huge, 450-square-foot deck that wrapped halfway around the house, and Tim loved grilling on the deck and having friends and family over. Unfortunately, we didn't have as many friends as we would have liked, as this was in the hills of Virginia, about thirty miles away from Charlottesville.

For exercise and sunshine, Tim and I walked around the city of Waynesboro almost every day. There was not much to see. Downtown stores and coffee shops closed at 5 pm, according to small town "rules." We had to travel 2-3 hours to go anywhere to see a concert or even to get to the beach.

The following November, we took a Norwegian ship cruise for a week to South Beach, Miami and the Bahamas. It might sound like this was not a big deal, but it was, because I have always been deathly afraid of the water. However, I had not really informed Tim. He had decided to surprise me with this trip, as we had never really had the chance for full honeymoon. I decided that as long as he was there, I could do anything that I set my mind to, and I really wanted to get over my fear.

Once we got on the cruise, I could not believe how beautiful it was. I didn't get anxious. I even went out to the balcony and looked at the big waves. It was so peaceful. After we came home, I finally told Tim how deathly afraid of the water I was. He couldn't believe how well I did.

He said, "Why didn't you tell me before we went?"

"Because it's time to experience the things I fear, and get over them. And it worked," I said.

My new husband treated me so well. He took me to fancy restaurants, to concerts, shows, pulled out chairs for me, and opened doors for me. I felt uncomfortable sometimes, because I was not used to it. Tim kept telling me, "Enjoy. Let me do it." He said I deserved it. I thought this was too good to be true. I still felt some uneasiness, because everything was like a dream. But over time, Tim convinced me it was all real. He cooked delicious meals, cleaned the house, did laundry and made sure the kids picked up after themselves.

I took an interior decorating course, became a certified interior decorator and learned how to decorate the house. I learned my colors, and started by putting new ceramic tiles and countertops in the kitchen. I painted every room a different color, and loved every second of it. I pulled the carpet off the stairs, sanded the wood underneath and stained them beautifully. Tim told me that he admired all my new renovations and helped whenever I needed it.

After all the work was done, we invited my brothers and all of my family from Northern Virginia for a big party. My brothers actually came and my cousins were there, too. Tim grilled and had fun. My brothers didn't directly converse with Tim, but they were polite, and everyone had a good time.

~~~

The girls, now aged fifteen, thirteen and twelve, had arguments at times, slamming doors, running up and down stairs and throwing dishes in the sink. They would go from being happy go-lucky to screaming and yelling in two seconds flat. In other words, they were being normal teenage girls.

We assigned chores for them, which they had to be reminded of a few times before they decided to do it. Unfortunately, Tim's two girls had some issues with trusting me as their stepmom. They never had had a strong female role model in their lives, and the never got used to having a mother to go to for support or advice. They had to learn how to communicate with me.

Tim had to remind them to trust me and talk to me if they needed to, but there were still times they wanted to talk to their dad about every little issue, like what to have for snack. I concentrated on being happy and patient most of the time, but there were times that I felt like I couldn't reach anyone, including my own daughter. Zohra was now about to turn sixteen and was very troubled. She was still depressed and didn't enjoy life at all.

We put Jay and the girls into counseling. I think Jay liked it, mostly because the counselor gave him treats every visit. But this made an inroad to the point that he would actually ask when his next visit to the counselor was. She earned his trust and had him opening up about things in no time.

The girls, on the other hand, were not too compliant with their counseling. But Tim was a better counselor to all of them than anyone else. He was so patient and calm, and helped the kids figure out things for themselves. He encouraged them to open up and just talk. It seemed like communication had opened up for all of us for the first time in our lives.

We both still had to deal with our ex-spouses and their visitations with the kids. After a while, his girls decided that they didn't want to have regular visits with their mother. The judge agreed, since they were old enough to make this decision for themselves. Zohra didn't visit her dad on a regular basis and Jay's visits didn't last long, since his dad was in and out of the country all of the time.

Whenever Dean was back in town, without warning, he would suddenly want to see Jay. This made things very unpredictable. Dean could talk with Tim just fine, and get things straightened out. But with me, it was a different story. Dean would get mad at me over the phone, and hang up on me. I would have to keep calling him to try to reach an agreement, and by that time, I would be very upset.

Jay asked me, "Why do Americans remain friends when they get a divorce, but not Afghans?" I told him that it was because divorce is not common in Afghan culture. The men just don't know how to deal with it.

During this time, I managed to not only work full time, but also become interested in massage therapy, especially as a way to help my obstetrics patients relax during the birthing process. Tim, once again, encouraged me to do whatever I wanted to do. The massage classes went as well as I had hoped, and twelve months later, I was a certified massage therapist, in addition to being a Registered Nurse. I immediately put my new skills to work, and it felt so good to be able to not only help women go through the difficult process of birthing, but to also help ease their pain.

~ Twenty-Three ~

Return to Kabul, 25 Years later

In the early 1980s, when we became political refugees in Istanbul, we were told that we could not go back to Afghanistan until we became American citizens. We were told that we would have to wait at least five years. It was in the late 1980s, while I was married to Dean, that I finally took the citizenship test and became a US citizen. By that time, the Russians had left Afghanistan, but the Mujahidin were in control. That was when fighting was at its worst. By 1996, the Taliban had taken control. Not only were we scared to go back to Kabul during these years, but such a trip would have been financially difficult for us.

Meanwhile, in Kabul, everyone had been forced to leave our family home. Our house was located near Bala Hissar, the ancient fortress, which was now a military target. Around 1995, some of my half brothers and sisters went to live in our relatives' villages – Shewakee and Benehisar – with our uncles, before the Taliban took over Kabul. Most of the rest of my family fled to the northern part of Kabul, and rented a big house together near a town called Taimany.

By 1997, some family members had returned home. The situation was getting worse, but they still had faith in the Taliban, and hoped that they would put an end to the fighting. Other family members started thinking of fleeing to Pakistan.

By the year 2000, most of Dean's family was living in Peshawar, Pakistan, and so was my oldest sister, Pari, and her six children. Dean, little Jay and I were able to afford a trip to Pakistan to see them that year. Zohra stayed behind with my brother Amir. All of my sisters and brothers who were still living in Kabul came to Peshawar to see me. It had been twenty years since either Dean or I had seen our families. We stayed a whole month. It was shocking to see them. They looked so old. Now my brothers wore the long beards, turbans, long shirts, and baggy pants that were required by the Taliban. All the women were now wearing *chaderi* – none of the skirts and blouses that we used to wear in the 1960s and 1970s. Women were not supposed to show their hands, feet or faces now; no skin. Women just did not go outside at all anymore, in order to be safe.

My family told me that there was lots of fighting going on, they had a curfew, and they weren't allowed to possess any entertainment – no radios, no TVs. The Taliban went around to homes enforcing their rules. If they found books, photo albums, or cameras, they burned them. Windows had to be painted black or have black curtains. It was worse than being in prison.

They told me a story about a woman who was out in the street, holding her baby. She was wearing a *chaderi*, but she wasn't accompanied by a man. A Talib shot her on the spot.

Women were also beaten with *shalaque*, a kind of cable made out of hard wire wrapped with leather. Zaybah said she was going with her daughter and her friend to the post office to make a phone call, because none of the phones were working. She and her friend were wearing *chaderi*s but her little 8-year-old daughter was wearing a pantsuit with a scarf around her neck (not covering her head). A

Talib started beating them both with a *shalaque*.

She didn't understand why. She said to the Talib, "Why are you beating me?"

The Talib said, "You think you're in America or something? This is a Muslim country. You shouldn't have your daughter out without a scarf on her head."

A man who was witnessing this said, "Run, go home, before he beats you more!" She grabbed her little girl, got in a cab and went home.

Rona said she went to buy a purse. She was wearing her *chaderi*. But she couldn't see through the *chaderi*'s little net in front of her eyes, so she lifted the front of the *chaderi* to see what she was buying. A Talib started hitting her on the back of her neck for lifting up her *chaderi*, and he also started hitting the male shopkeeper for letting her expose her face while shopping. Rona didn't know what to do, and started crying. The shopkeeper told her to leave, since he got in trouble too. Rona went home and didn't go shopping again for as long as the Taliban were in power. My heart ached at the thought of them going through so much torture.

I got to see Sohaila. Her sister had moved to Pakistan, too. Sohaila was very frail – her husband had been in the military and was killed during the war, and she took it badly. She was very sick, and told me, "I'll probably be dead by the next time you come."

I always used to have nightmares of the Mujahidin (and later the Taliban) chasing my family and me with guns for not being covered from head to toe or for some other reason. I would wake up with my heart racing, and covered in sweat. Those dreams have been disappearing lately. I have to give thanks to my husband Tim for teaching me how to recover from those dreams and how to control my bad dreams and wake myself up. It really works, for I have decided that there will be no more nightmares of war for me.

Me in Peshawar, Pakistan in 2000.

~~~

After fleeing Kabul for a few years, eventually my youngest brother
Aman and his family were able to return to our dad's house. The roof
had been burnt, windows were broken, and all our family pictures
were gone, but they rebuilt the family home.

Tim knew how much I wanted to see my family. So, in May
2005, he booked a ticket for me to go to Kabul. I had not been

back since I fled from Kabul as a refugee, and twenty-five years had passed. I was very excited, yet scared, to go back to the place I had escaped from, after Russia invaded Afghanistan. For the first time, I was going back to the land where I was raised.

I started crying as soon as the plane flew over the city of Kabul and landed. I saw first-hand how the Taliban had destroyed our country; how the trees had all been burned, and how streets and buildings had been torn apart by land mines and bombs. Even though it was spring, the air was so dusty. People said it hadn't rained since the Taliban had arrived. The people of Afghanistan believed that since there was so much killing and bloodshed, God must be unhappy with them. They prayed for the souls of those killed by the Taliban. They constantly prayed to God for forgiveness, even though it wasn't their fault.

I went to my family home. I had never met Aman's six children before – and they were beautiful. They kept calling me *Ama-jaan* (father's sister – dear aunt). I met Zaybah's and Rona's kids too, who called me *Khala-jaan* (mother's sister - dear aunt).

A ton of people gathered there just to see me, including my half brothers, half sisters, and about fifty or sixty nieces and nephews. They did not stop having children even though they were living in the middle of the war. All these kids grew up in a war zone, so they didn't know anything but war, bombs and killing of innocent people. They weren't afraid of anything. The people of Afghanistan didn't have complete freedom yet, but at least the Taliban were gone now. They were very appreciative of being able to go out of the house without fear of being shot at or hit by a Talib. They could now listen to their music, watch TV, take pictures and have wedding and engagement parties.

Zaman and Ria came to Afghanistan as well, and joined us a little later. The bond between all the kids was growing closer; living so far away from each other had made us appreciate each other more.

Afghans are the most hospitable people in the world. They always make sure they serve their guests the best of what they have. Here I was, wishing that I could help them, but instead, they were spending what little money they had to provide a five-course meal, without a second thought. It made me feel guilty and spoiled.

~~~

In 2005, the streets were crowded with Afghans coming back from the refugee camps in Iran, Pakistan, India, and Russia. Women were back on the streets without wearing *chaderi*s; they just covered their heads with a big scarf, and showed their faces. They weren't afraid anymore, since the Taliban was gone. At least that is what they thought.

This was the second time I saw my sister Zaybah since we went to Pakistan five years earlier, and she looked better. Everyone looked happier and healthier, with more life in their eyes, because the Taliban was gone.

I went to my mother's grave with my sister Zaybah. I sat there for the longest time. I didn't know what to say to my mother and father after all these years; I had never had a chance to say goodbye.

It had been a lifetime of separation, though it still seemed as if I had just seen them yesterday. I decided to keep it simple. I told them, "I am OK, and I'm happy." I felt a sense of calm and comfort. I sensed that my parents were not upset with me for marrying an American man.

My mother was buried in a simple grave, with only a little tombstone and nothing on it; but my uncle knew who was buried where. During the war, landmines destroyed many graves, including hers. So before I left, I made sure that both my mom and dad's graves were fixed up, with a tombstone and concrete put around them to honor and protect their memories.

I went to Shewakee (my mom's village) to see my youngest sister, Rona, the one that was married off at age sixteen. She ended up having elelven children. Rona's oldest daughter, Fawzia, married around age seventeen and now had seven daughters of her own. She looked so frail and vulnerable, holding her youngest baby. A full-time, uneducated mother – she looked as if she had the weight of the world on her shoulders. Her husband was preparing bricks to build their own home, but for now, they were all living in a single room at her parents' home. Imagine, if you can, nine people living in one room: one room in which to eat, sleep and play. This is the normal state of things after years of oppression, war, and poverty.

My niece Fawzia turned out to be the most loving person, though. Her eyes were beaming at me, smiling. I remember when she was only four or five years old. I delivered her younger brother. She asked me, "How is it possible that you can come all the way to Afghanistan by yourself?" She was amazed to see her American aunt and the freedom that I represented to her.

My sisters Zaybah, Rona and I, were sitting with the rest of the family inside having tea in the afternoon, and we heard a lot of noise outside. We all rushed outside to see what was going on. Fawzia's 18-month-old daughter had been pushed by her older brother onto the concrete in the front yard. We found her unconscious. I looked at the pale, unresponsive child with blue lips lying on the ground. The mother and the grandmother and everyone started wailing, "She's dead, she's dead!" They were all gathered around her. I made my way through the crowd, and managed to pick her up and take her inside. I laid her gently on the floor. She was not breathing, so I gave her two ventilating breaths. She had a pulse. Then I give her two more ventilating breaths. She started to cough and her little body started to wiggle.

Her mother and everyone were cheering and thanking me for saving the child. They didn't know exactly what I did, and said that I blew into her mouth and brought her back to life. I explained to them what I did. They were in awe. I told them, "If your children went to school, they would know what do to, too." Fawzia came to me and hugged me, sobbing and thanking me for saving her daughter. My sister Rona was so appreciative.

Rona was actually the smartest of all of us. And brave. It still shocked me that she had been taken out of school at the age of sixteen, and married off to my cousin. After that, she had a child every year for the next eleven years. I wondered just what kind of profession she could have had, given half a chance.

Rona actually almost bled to death while giving birth to her eighth child at home, in Shewakee. Her sister-in-law did nothing, and just watched as her condition deteriorated. Finally, Rona's ten-year-old son took a two-hour bus ride to our home in Kabul to tell Amir and Pari what was going on. They immediately took a cab to the village, and when they arrived, she was almost dead. They transported her on her blood-saturated mattress in the back of the cab to the hospital where she received blood transfusions. I have to say here and now that it must have been God who saved her.

I kept pushing Rona and Fawzia very hard to send Fawzia's younger kids to school, especially since they couldn't send them under the Taliban's rule.

"The Taliban are gone. I am begging you to do this one thing for me. Remember, it was my education and God that saved your grandchild," I told Rona.

She agreed with me, but said, "It's my son who won't allow the girls to go to school." It was the son that I remembered delivering, about twenty-six years ago.

"Well," I said, "If that's the case, then you can teach them at home first. That will benefit you, too."

"I'm too old, and I have no patience," she said.

So I went and I spoke with her son about it. After some debate, he finally agreed with me that this was indeed a good thing to do.

I felt a sense of accomplishment; I felt that the girls of the current generation might actually have a chance after all. I had not shirked away from my responsibilities and was surprised as well by how I was being viewed by the younger men of the family.

~ Twenty-Four ~

A Second Trip Home

Two years later, I made my second trip home to Afghanistan. The decision to visit my family again so soon was sudden. My stepmom Zewar had died. I was trying not to get too emotional about it at first, since it was Christmastime. My brother's family was supposed to have dinner with us, and Tim and I were occupied with all the necessary arrangements.

The news of my stepmom's death came when my oldest brother called. "Zewar died," he said. He told me, "I think it's best we cancel our dinner – we shouldn't have a party at this time."

"How about we just gather together and have a service for her?" I suggested.

"No, if we gather on Christmas it will seem like we're having a party," he said. I was distraught. I needed to be with my brothers and my family at that time.

We all cared for Zewar since she was part of the family. I called and talked to all my brothers and sisters in Kabul. My family was together there, mourning her passing, and I felt so alone. I started sobbing, since my brothers weren't even going to join me for dinner.

I tried to put on a brave face for my husband and children on Christmas day. But Tim could see right through me.

He said, "Are you going to be OK?"

"I was thinking, if only I could be with all my family in Afghanistan. Then I might be OK," I said.

Tim looked at me and said, "You are going. I want you to be with your family."

He said he would arrange for my flight and everything. I was hesitant at first, because of the cost and the long flight, but it sounded like it was the right thing to do. I agreed.

My boss and coworkers made sure I could take some time off from work. Ria came to see me the day I left, and that made me feel better.

I did manage to see my brothers before I left. We talked about Zewar. Her death brought back a lot of memories, both good and bad. She was the last part of our childhood saga, and the unhappy history of sharing my father with her and my half siblings. We talked about how it was so amazing to see that now, my dad's thirteen children, eight-seven grandchildren and over fifty great-grandchildren lived all over the world – in Afghanistan, America, Canada, Germany and London.

When we had visited our family in Afghanistan in 2005, Zewar was very happy to see us. She had always shown us her affection by hugging and sweet-talking. She said, "You're like my children and I love you like my own children. Your mom was like a sister to me." We all treated her well and respected her, as we really did understand that none of what had happened had anything to do with her; it was just the circumstances that we all found ourselves in.

All of Zewar's kids live in Afghanistan. The girls were less educated than we were, and they got married very young. They didn't have a chance to finish school, or to learn about the world at all. Each one of them had between six and eight children by now. They ended up with a lot of dental problems and health issues.

Their husbands were less educated, too. Their kids grew up during the Taliban years, and therefore no education was provided for them – least of all for the girls. Again, I tried to encourage them to educate their children, now that they had the chance, and got them some notebooks, pens, pencils and coloring books and crayons.

My half brothers did finish college. Unfortunately, my youngest half brother was taken by the Mujahidin and forced to fight, and was killed. Zewar was devastated over the loss of her son. She visited his grave almost everyday.

Zaybah's and Aman's kids were all educated and continued on to become lawyers and teachers, which always gives me such pride. Their parents value education. I have tried so many times to persuade the rest of my half sisters and their kids to further their education, but unfortunately I still haven't succeeded.

~~~

On this trip, for Zewar's memorial, I found myself waiting at 2 am at the Dubai International Airport to catch my Kam Air flight to Kabul. When I finally got to Kabul, I saw that a lot had changed from just two years earlier. I noticed it first from high above Kabul in the airplane, and then when I got off. Everywhere I looked, there was new construction, and new signs of life. I felt good about it all.

Half of the passengers on the plane were Americans and aid workers. They seemed quieter and more reserved than most of the Americans that I have ever known. They were more familiar with our customs, and the women had headscarves ready when they departed the plane.

My nephew, my sister Zaybah and my brother Aman greeted me at the airport. I was very emotional and excited to see them. We went to my family home where I was greeted by my half brothers and sisters. Above all else, I wanted to show my sympathy with them for the death of my stepmother.

The memorial service was at Zewar's oldest son's house, our first family home. The custom is for the memorial to last several days. Zewar had already been buried when I arrived, as tradition says that the body is to be buried within twenty-four hours. Close family members sat and drank tea while people visited. Everyone talked about our good memories. I sat with my half sisters in a row on the floor, and visitors came to pay their respects to us. I arrived during the fifth day of the memorial, and things had calmed down a little by then. But people were still coming to pay their respects, and I saw a lot of people I had not seen in ages. They came and told their sad war stories.

Zewar's oldest daughter was not getting along with her brothers. She seemed bothered by some of the little details of the service, and ended up arguing with her oldest brother and didn't come back. Unfortunately I did not get to see her again.

Everyone seemed very sad, but excited to see me at the same time. They appreciated me for coming from so far away to the service and to see them. I felt so close to them. It felt right that I could be with my family to share in their sorrow and our memories.

I spent the rest of my trip at Zaybah's, and Rona, my youngest sister, also stayed at Zaybah's the entire time I was there. She kept staring at me, amazed just to see me. I entertained the kids by taking pictures of them doing little things, and getting them to pose for the camera. They dressed up and loved getting ready for their poses. I constantly applauded them for living in that situation and hanging in there. I told them, "You are my heroes."

They only had electricity at night for about three hours, but they knew what to do without power, and kept their home warm with gas and wood stoves and bathed in buckets of warm water. Of course, I did the same things they did, even to the point of sitting on the floor with them. Soon enough though, my knees would complain and I had to stretch my legs.

~~~

I visited my uncle Khan's house in the suburbs of Kabul, near the mountains, which is located near my maternal cemetery. That's where my grandmother, grandfather, oldest uncle, *Mami* and the rest of the clan are buried. My uncle visits them every day and prays on their graves. He told me, "Your mother is happy and cared for. Do not worry about her." He held my hands and talked and prayed with me as I went to *Mami*'s grave. I still couldn't believe she was gone. My mom is still always alive in my dreams. I never went through the grieving process, and didn't want to. But it gave me a sense of peace, just being at her graveside and talking to her that day.

I started talking to my mother as if she were sitting right next to me. I spoke to her about being married to an American. I told her that he was a very kind, sensitive gentleman, and how happy I was with my husband. I asked my mother for her forgiveness, as I had always felt guilty for not making it back before her death, and I wanted her to know how I felt.

I did the same thing when I visited my father's grave. My father was worried about me before he died. He told Zaybah that he was concerned about me being in America, all alone and unmarried. This day, I assured him that I was married to a very nice, caring and loving man, and that I was very happy. I couldn't do this the last time I came to visit his grave.

Then, I went to Zewar's grave. I was sad to lose her. Zewar was part of the good and sad part of my past, and I couldn't help but sob for the loss of that entire generation. The last time I came, Zewar was happy to see me and accompanied me everywhere. She prayed for me all the time. She appreciated the little gifts I brought her last time – some fabric for a dress and a white scarf.

Suddenly, I was able to forget and forgive Zewar for all the grief she had given my mother. I felt close to her. There was no reason to hate her. She was old and had been nice to us. She had suffered enough through the years, and now it was time to show her respect.

~~~

A few years earlier, I had started sponsoring a child through an international charity called Afghan Child Education and Care Organization. I wanted to meet my sponsored child, and started looking for the orphanage in Kabul. It took me a while to find the place, since there are about twenty orphanages in Kabul. I had to contact my husband in the US, ask him to email the head of the orphanage. I received an email and contacted her, and it worked out well, especially since no one in Kabul knew where the orphanage was located. (This is actually a good thing in Kabul, as the lower the profile of an orphanage, the more likely it is to succeed).

I went to the orphanage and met all of the children, except my child. Apparently, she had gone to visit her family during Eid (the Muslim celebration after Ramadan) and had not returned yet. That didn't stop me from visiting the other kids, and talking to them and enjoying their jokes, and shaking their little hands and touching their heads and hugging them. All the other kids had sponsors except one. I asked the director if I could adopt her as well, and I got approval.

So now, I was sponsoring two 13-year old girls.

My second child couldn't stop smiling as I shook her hand and hugged her as tightly as I could. That made my day, my month and my year.

I took pictures with the kids and saw their neatly made bunk beds and arranged rooms, and I told them I admired them for their courage and their hard work. I told them to get along, become educated and to become somebody; to help rebuild the country and help bring peace. Their little heads nodded in agreement. Nothing made me happier than to see these kids with their bright, curious eyes full of excitement, eager to see this sponsor from America. I wanted to pack them all on a bus to take them home with me. I would have given them the world if I could have, and I truly felt that they knew this. They melted my heart, and they also reminded me of just how strong I was…because they *were* me.

I wanted to do the same thing with my little nieces and nephews. They all were so precious, gathered around me every day. That made me appreciate my family and friends more, and I found myself wanting to be the role model that they envision me to be. I bought the kids notebooks, pencils and pens, clothes, money, lipsticks and gave them all lots of love. We laughed and cried for our country. I then realized that I was just like my mother; I wanted the best for everyone.

~~~

The day came when it was time to go back to the US. I talked with Tim on the phone that morning and missed him terribly; I always miss my husband and kids when I am away. I had loved being back in Kabul, but I couldn't wait to get back home.

Now I had to say goodbye to everyone, which is always the hardest part to do. All of my family members brought me dried fruit and green tea to take home for my brothers and me. My nieces made me a couple of Afghan comforters, which were the hardest things to pack, for they were actually velvet-patched quilts, made for twin and queen-sized beds. It had taken them days to finish.

I made it to the airport, but the person at the check-in told me that my bags were overweight and that I had to pay extra for them. Unfortunately, I had no money for this, as I had spent all my money to help others. I only had twenty-five dollars that my nephew had given me, and they didn't take credit cards. After almost an hour, I managed to convince the very last person at the check-in counter that I had no money, and I actually made it on the plane just a minute before it left.

I sat next to an important gentleman from the Afghan government. I really enjoyed conversing with him and didn't notice how fast the time passed. Then we arrived in Dubai, at 4 pm, where I had to wait for my flight to San Francisco, leaving at 7:40 am.

I now had all night to kill. I was afraid to spend the last thirty dirhams I had, but I did manage to buy a bottle of water and a salad, and still had five dirhams left over. I found someone at the airport to loan me an adapter to charge my computer, since mine had round prongs and not flat (if you have never travelled overseas, one word of advice: find out what kind of plugs they use!) and spent part of the night writing.

Finally, the morning came. Again, I stood in line waiting to check my luggage. I had three bags instead of two, and as a result, they told me that I had to go back and have two of my bags wrapped together. I had my bags wrapped, and the person charged me twenty dirhams. But I only had five left. So I hurried to a bank to try to get some cash. True to my luck at the end of this trip, the bank would not give me a cash advance, because my card happened to be in my husband's name, and I didn't have my ATM card. I then went to a store to see if I could purchase something and get cash back. Nothing was working, and I started to panic.

Time was running out. I went back to the bank and was so upset that I point-blank told those Arab men to give me a break. I actually started yelling at them for not helping me. "Here I am, in a foreign country, a woman on her own, literally stuck and you are not lifting a finger to help!" I yelled. (Islam does not allow this, as any self-respecting man knows, he would offend God if he turned his back on a helpless woman).

They looked at me as if I was losing my mind. No other woman would ever talk to them like that. One of them asked me, "How much do you need?" And I told him. He pulled out fifteen dirhams (which is about $5) and handed it to me. At that point, all I could say was, "Thank you," and walk away. I had to rush back to my bags and get back in line to check them in.

I got to the boarding gate to catch my flight, and right then and there, I missed my husband. I thought, if he had been there, nothing like that would have happened to me. I promised myself that I would never travel without him again.

I was glad to get back to Dulles airport and thanked God to be back in America. I was so happy to see Tim at the airport. He hadn't shaved the whole time I was gone. I hugged him and did not want to let go. I could not help myself – I had to snap a picture of his unshaven, gruffly face.

It was good to be home again and to see my husband and the kids. They kept saying, "It's good to have you home, because we were all walking around aimlessly, and didn't know what to do.

There was no mommy to tell us to do this and that, and come eat."
It was good to be missed.

After a trip, I always have hard time getting back into our routine. But after a few months, I got on with our normal life and felt lucky to be here in this country. Life here is so much easier than what the Afghan people have to go through. Just taking a hot shower is a blessing, driving a car to work, not to mention having electricity twenty-four hours a day. People constantly complain about the little things that make no sense, and waste so much food and water.

The economy in Afghanistan is worse than anyone in the States could ever imagine. They don't have enough money to buy food, never mind the extra stuff we spend money on and take for granted, from the time we get up to the time we go to sleep.

~ Twenty-Five ~

Living in California

In September 2007, my husband and I started thinking of relocating. We tried to find jobs in California first, since we both had lived there before. I had my heart set on San Diego, but a potential job fell through, and the wildfires blazing in San Diego crushed our dream. Tim suggested Florida, but I was not too crazy about that, since his ex-wife lived there. He reassured me that there would be plenty of distance from her, and that there wouldn't be any contact. Oh, the warm weather and the thought of relaxing at the beach in Florida were tempting.

In February of 2008, I found myself sitting in the lobby of Palmetto Medical Center in Florida where my husband had his first job interview. Tim had two different hospitals vying for him. The lobby was full of visitors going in and out, mostly speaking Spanish, and it was obvious that the area had a huge Latin American population. I was thinking that if we did get jobs here, learning Spanish might be necessary.

The offers did not come, and it was devastating. It turned out that Tim's personality was too strong for one of the positions, and at the other hospital, the CEO refused to hire him because he was from out of state.

Then, on the way back from seeing a recruiter, he received a call. It seemed that there was a job in Northern California for a radiology director position that would be perfect for Tim. He asked me not to get my hopes up, but for some reason, he seemed to have a quiet confidence about him that I had not seen since we started looking.

It turned out that Tim got a great offer in San Ramon, California, as director of radiology. I ended up getting a job as a labor and delivery nurse at the same hospital. He was very excited, and so was I. We had always wanted to live in California and our wish had come true. When it came time to pack we had to make a big decision: either get rid of stuff or spend $12,000 to move it. We also had to put the house on the market.

Tim and I were working our full time jobs and packing at home, and we were exhausted. We didn't have much help, other than a couple we hired to help us clean the house and the yard. I wished my sisters were here. Zaybah loves to help and pack. That is something I always missed – my sisters. My sister in-law Ria and my youngest nephew came one day and helped, which I really appreciated.

It took about a month to get everything done. Fortunately, we successfully got rid of all the furniture and clutter. We moved on Saturday March 21st, which was actually the Afghan New Year. It was the perfect way to start the New Year.

Amir got upset with me for moving to California. Zohra was at university by this time, and she was going to stay in Virginia. He questioned me about Zohra, about the house and everything else. He said every single thing possible, except that he would miss me and wished me luck. What hurt me the most was that when it all happened, it was my birthday. I had just turned fifty, but I felt like my brothers were still treating me like a two-year-old.

I didn't let it bother me. My life has turned around ever since I married Tim. I have the confidence and happiness I never had before. Even my coworkers and friends have noticed and spoken about the difference in me.

I know if my mom and dad were alive today, they would be proud of me and admire the courage and confidence I have now. My dad always wanted me to be a doctor (which in our culture would have been amazing for a girl). I told my daughter Zohra, "If I were about five years younger, I would go to medical school just for my dad, and I would retire after that."

~~~

We packed up my Jeep Liberty and loaded whatever we could into a 15-foot trailer that we towed all the way from Virginia to California. We took our cats, Blizzard and Honey, in cat carriers in the truck, because we didn't want them to have heart attacks on the plane. Jay wanted to ride along to be with Honey, the kitten we adopted from the SPCA. Honey is his baby, and they grew up together.

The longest part of the trip was through Kansas and hundreds of miles of farmland. I slept a lot. Tim drove most of the way, and I was glad he could do it. When we stopped in Kansas after day two, Tim was dead tired. After not seeing a town for 100 miles, we finally found one. We pulled up to two hotels, which were both booked. It became apparent that we had stopped in a military town, and the first of the troops from operation "Iraqi Freedom" were returning home.

We stopped at the last hotel, hoping beyond hope. "We don't have a room," they said. The next town was another seventy-five miles. Tim pleaded with them. They looked again and found a room that someone had booked, but had not shown up for. They took pity on us and gave it to us.

Tim was bringing stuff up to the room, and decided to bring Blizzard and Honey up. Imagine, it's Kansas, 20 degrees in April, and Tim is carrying two cat carriers. As he gets to the second floor, I see the bottom fall out of one of the carriers and Blizzard comes out flying. I hear Tim screaming, "Blizzard…stop!!!" and he's running after Blizzard as fast as he can on the catwalk of the second floor. It was a sight beyond all sights. It was suddenly over, when Blizzard realized that he "wasn't in Virginia anymore," and stopped. It makes me chuckle to this day.

We were on the road for five days. We stopped at hotels and rested, and in the mornings, we had to get Honey out from under the bed. Blizzard, on the other hand, always wanted to be outside all night.

We arrived in California on April 11, 2008. We instantly felt at home and immediately took to the area.

~~~

It was like a dream, driving up to 305 Beal Drive, in Santa Cruz, California. This was where I had lived with my host family thirty years ago, as a young nurse-midwife student. The streets looked so unfamiliar and familiar at the same time.

We took the winding road through the woods, arrived at the empty house, and stopped at the closed gate. There was a sign, "be aware of dogs," that made me uncomfortable. Of course, my hosts didn't live there anymore – they had moved a couple years after I stayed with them.

It was déjà vu, as the house was on the market again. This time it was different, though, as I was with my husband. He was standing by my side and supporting me. He told me to get out of the car and take a good look at the house, to remember the past, and get it out of my system.

I said, "It feels so weird. I never thought I would ever come back here again." I picked up a brochure from the real estate box; it priced the house at over two and a half million dollars.

I was amazed at how much the surroundings had changed. Oh my God, I remembered my best friend Sohaila, who was by my side at all times and who treated me like her daughter. We rode our bikes together and cried, missing our families. We went shopping together and on and on. I remembered when I fell off the bicycle and hurt myself. Now, I could barely handle thinking of Sohaila, it made me so sad.

I had tried to visit Sohaila when I was in Afghanistan in 2005. I called one of my friends, and asked for her address. She told me, "I'm sorry Anisa, Sohaila passed away a couple of months ago." I couldn't believe it. But, at the same time, I had become used to hearing that kind of news. My nephew and I managed to find her sister's house, and she and I hugged and cried for a long time. It was so strange to see her sister without Sohaila. They always used to be together.

I stood in front of my host's house for a few minutes, just remembering old times. Then Tim and I got in to the car, and went home.

~~~

I started my new job after a couple of weeks. I had to start from square one, getting oriented to the obstetrics floor. I liked the people I worked with – for the most part they were helpful, and the patient population was more diverse than in Virginia.

I loved the area. I loved being able to go for long walks in the mornings, then go to the gym with Tim and the kids. The kids were still homebodies. They didn't want to go out much, and it took a lot of persuasion to get them out.

The housing in Northern California was very expensive. We looked for some houses to buy, but could not believe the prices: three-quarters of a million dollars for a decent-sized house in a good neighborhood. There were actually no houses on the market with even the minimum requirements for a price that we could afford. We stopped looking and decided to rent. Besides, we still had a house back in Virginia to sell. Sometimes we talked about keeping the house there, and going back once we retired. It would be much cheaper.

Due to the move, I had to get my permanent California nursing license, which again required the huge hurdle of requesting my nursing school transcripts. I had to contact my sister Zaybah in Afghanistan to get my transcripts. We had graduated together in 1976. Fortunately, her husband worked for the ministry of health. He could get access to my profile, and assured me that he would be able to get my transcripts. In the meantime, I had to sit and wait.

I still couldn't believe how wonderfully I was being treated at home. One night, I attended a bridal shower with some of my coworkers, and went to dinner and dancing after. I enjoyed it very much. My wonderful husband came and picked me up at 1 am, and even let me sleep the next day as long as I could. He then went and fixed chili for the kids and my friends at work. After I got off work the next morning, I found the garage clicker and a note posted to it. It read, "You are close to my heart and being loved with its complete essence. Have a beautiful day my Angel! Yours Forever, T."

That is what keeps me going – knowing that someone cares as deeply for me as I do for him. I get up every day and thank God for my health and my family's well being, for being alive and for having a loving husband and children. In addition, we live in the most beautiful state of California. (I call it Little Heaven). The weather is gorgeous, and I enjoy the sunshine every day. Even the winters are beautiful in Northern California. The sound of the pouring rain is soothing, as Blizzard sleeps by Tim's feet.

My husband keeps saying, "What did I do to deserve you?" I could say the same thing every day. I am living in a country where I have my freedom, a job that pays well, and we have food on the table. I could not ask for more. Some days I feel like I am in a dream. I have to pinch myself to see if I'm awake.

~~~

Work was challenging, but I learned to be proactive, to stand up for myself when I needed something, and to be a good advocate for my patients. I could not and would not have done that six years ago. There is nothing in the world that scares me anymore. What a change for a shy, phobic person! What happened to that scared person that could not speak up in a group? She does show up, once in awhile, but not as often. I only wish that I could have been this brave when I was younger.

By searching on the Web, I found out that there is actually a condition called Spasmodic Voice. I had suffered from this condition for years and years, and was hoping beyond hope that there was something that could be done to improve my tight, cracking, hoarse voice that made me very self-conscious most of the time. This was the main reason I became phobic and anxious to read or speak in public, and I wanted a cure. I made an appointment to go to my doctor and get a referral for a speech therapist. She gave me exercises to help strengthen the muscles around my vocal chords, which proved helpful.

At first, I thought that I had wasted most of my life worrying about stuff. I thought, "If only I knew as much then as I do now." The more I thought about it, though, the more I realized that those things have brought me to where I am, who I am, and who I am with. I rediscovered that life is not about things; it is about happiness and treasuring every moment of every second. That is what I decided to hold on to from now on. There is nothing more beautiful than my husband sleeping here next to me.

I thank God then, for those trials. I am grateful of all life's lessons that I have learned, and for the opportunity to do so. Most people go through a lifetime and they still don't get it.

~~~

I started getting used to my job and making friends. In September 2008, I decided to open up a massage therapy office, since I was only working two days a week at the hospital. I had no earthly idea how it was going to go, but I was excited nonetheless.

When I opened up my massage office, I didn't think I would have any customers. But people came, and kept coming because they were happy with my massage technique. It also did not hurt that I was a registered nurse, and they immediately knew that I would do them no harm. I enjoyed doing massage, and the good feeling of helping someone.

My office was beautifully decorated in very simple and serene themes. It was small, but private, and it was my own. I began feeling selfish and begged God, "Please forgive me." I learned a lot about business, and even designed and ordered my own business cards and brochures. Then I began to get regular clients. Massage is my kind of work. I can relax someone with my touch, and alleviate stress with my warm, healing hands. I want to help people forget about their hard day and relax. That is my mission.

~~~

That year, Tim's daughter Marin turned seventeen. I was happy for her. She had had a tough life, and I could not love a child more than I do her. It has never mattered for a second that she did not come from my womb. Nichole was nineteen and living on her own, and seemed so grown-up and appreciative of everything. And Zohra was twenty-one, and away at college in Virginia. I missed her terribly. And Jay was growing up, too. That summer, he went to camp for the first time.

In November 2008, on the fifth day of Eid, I called everyone to wish them a happy Eid, saying "*Eid-eh Shoma Mobarak.*" Then it was time for Christmas, and it was a beautiful one indeed. Zohra flew in from Richmond, Virginia and spent the entire week with us. She and Marin actually fixed us Christmas breakfast. We went shopping, to the gym, the movies, and on walks.

Then in July 2009, I lost my dear aunt Sofia to cancer. I couldn't believe she could die so soon. She suffered six years of massive pain and broken bones due to multiple myeloma (a type of bone marrow cancer). Her spine had to be surgically cemented together. Her middle son is a doctor, and he and his wife took good care of her. She was so lucky to have a son that was by her side during her times of pain and suffering. As I often say, it is obvious that what you do and how you treat people will come back to you, especially during the worst of times.

I still can't believe she is gone. She was not just my travelling companion when we fled Afghanistan; she was so much more than that. She became the closest person to me, especially during the last few years of her life. It was very hard to lose her.

Aunt Sofia was more traditional than the rest of the family. However, she was also the most understanding, open-minded and loving person I have known. She supported Tim and me at our wedding, even though she was sick and we didn't know it yet. After we found out about her illness, we visited her home in Virginia, and she made lunch for us. She asked Tim, "Will you pray to your God for me?" Which of course he then did, bringing us all to tears. She said, "Thank you."

The last time I saw her was in the hospital. I stayed with her for a few hours, and helped her bathe and shampoo her hair. She was very fragile and weak. Her bones were very brittle and painful. She was on heavy pain medication. She still had her sense of humor, though. She was the life of the party when she was younger. My mom loved her very much, and used to call her "the laughing flower."

She is survived by her husband, three grown sons, daughters-in-law, and nine grandchildren. Her husband is also very sick due to Parkinson's disease. She loved him to death. She would never leave his side when she was healthy. She treated him like a king, and their love was mutual.

As I was sitting on the plane returning from the funeral and the burial in Virginia, I couldn't help but sob for my dear, sweet aunt. First she lost her 19-year-old, only daughter in Germany in a minor surgery mishap, and then cancer robbed her of her happy and active life, slowly and painfully.

I looked out of the window on the plane, and saw the beautiful white fluffy clouds glittering with the sunshine.

I looked deeply into them. I could see my aunt holding her

daughter's hand. They were laughing and dancing on the clouds, waving at me. I felt comfort and peace as I waved back to them, knowing my aunt was with her only daughter, and she was happy.

~ Twenty-Six ~

Dreaming of Family

I am sitting in my kitchen with the backyard garden, looking at the yellow roses I picked out for the dining room table. I also got some tall lavender lantana flowers for the coffee table and for my meditation room. I am enjoying every second of their beauty. Tim is sitting in the living room playing a PS3 baseball game, enjoying his Sunday and relaxing before he goes back to work tomorrow. He comes into the kitchen every once in a while and gives me a kiss.

Jay is still sleeping. I tried to wake him up earlier, with no luck. He stays up late on weekends, so I guess he has to catch up on his sleep; just your typical 14-year-old boy.

He is such a great kid with so much talent and charisma, and very loyal to family and friends. He has joined the high school football team this summer, and he loves it. Time flies, and so does his growth. He is now suddenly 5'10" tall, lean and still growing like a weed. He is never full, though he tries to eat healthier now since he is playing football.

I can't believe he is going to high school this year. My baby is growing up. I have been spending more time with him at home, trying to capture every second that I can.

I do miss my daughter Zohra, she is so far away on the east coast. She graduated from college and currently works at Home Depot. She is planning on going to graduate school, but has not decided which one yet. She has a lot of typical young adult issues, but she keeps going, never afraid to ask for advice or help. She is growing up and making very good decisions in her life, and I am very proud of her.

She does call us, especially Tim for advice and suggestions. In a way, he is like a counselor to her, and he challenges her with problem solving issues. Most of the time, it is about relationships and male issues. She and I have grown extremely close, both via phone and text messages, and it makes me smile every time I see that it is her calling or texting.

Nichole is away, living on her own. I begin to dream about the day my husband and I will have grandchildren. Tim jokes, "Our grandchildren will be running around our house, and we'll send them home to their parents with their noisy toys." I only wish my parents could have been part of our children's lives today.

I remember how my mother used to gather up her grandchildren and reward them with their favorite food and snacks after she played with them. It makes me sad that she will never get to meet my five children, for I know she would have been a loving and generous grandmother. She would have adored our children, and they would have loved her very much.

This also reminds me of my grandmother, *Bebe-jaan*, who lived well into her nineties. She was very frail and very religious. She prayed five times a day and fasted often. She liked to sit on the second floor windowsill of her son's house in the mountainous region of Kabul, and soak up the sun and watch people coming and going throughout the day. Occasionally, my mother, Mariam, would bring her to our house for a visit. Her mind was sharp, and she didn't have any physical limitations. Even by today's standards, she was amazingly healthy, and she never had to take any medicine throughout her long life. I remember all the times when we as a family went to my uncle's house to visit her. I was around fifteen years old when she died of old age, and I suffered greatly from not seeing her again. I missed her gentle spirit and kind ways.

~ Twenty-Seven ~

A Third Trip to Afghanistan

In April 2010, I had another opportunity to go back to Afghanistan to visit my family, and I am glad I did. The reasons for this are many, but mainly because of my brother Aman. He is diabetic, and not getting the proper care in Kabul. He is getting very weak and his condition is worsening.

After we landed at Kabul airport, I was greeted by my brother Aman, his daughters, Suraya and Fareeda, my sister Rona and my cousin Waheed. We all packed into Waheed's van. They were all quizzing me about the names of the streets and buildings. They were actually very surprised by how much I remembered. We all had a good time on the way to Aman's house, which was originally my father's second home.

His wife and other kids fixed us lunch and tea, and we all gathered together, just like old times. It was so wonderful to see everyone. Aman looked frail and weak, especially compared with the last time I had seen him. His front teeth had discolored from diabetes. He told me his legs were weak and that he couldn't even feel them sometimes. He said that he would get dizzy and that he couldn't see well. I was very concerned to hear about these symptoms, because it definitely sounded like some neuropathy had developed. I insisted that my nephew check his blood sugar level, and it turned out to be 389. Normal is 70-120.

He was sitting with the guests, getting ready to eat dinner, but I didn't want him to eat, and insisted that he go to the doctor. I offered to go with him, but he didn't want me to. I will never understand the concept that Afghan men have of not wanting to go to the doctor accompanied by a woman. He asked his son Paiman to go with him. He came back with a bunch of medicine, including multivitamins, vitamin B12, and antibiotics. The next morning, he looked much better after taking his meds, and he did not appear nearly as weak.

The following day, we went on a picnic to beautiful Kharga Lake, which is surrounded by snow-covered mountains, green hills and picnic areas. Aman planned the food with his wife and kids that morning, and packed the teapots and rugs and everything we would need. He seemed excited. He appeared more energized and was laughing and having a good time. He made sure everything was perfect. My sister Zaybah, and her sons Emad and Ehsan joined us later on. We ate lamb kabobs, chicken kabobs, and other Afghan appetizers along with tea. I videotaped everyone and took pictures. We had a ball.

The area has changed so much since the last time I was there in 2005. Now cars are parked by the lake, there is horseback riding and kite flying everywhere, and boat rentals. The kids and adults were just having so much fun. That is the kind of happiness I want to see for our Afghan people. They deserve it; they don't need to suffer anymore.

We came back home to Aman's at 8 pm, to a bunch of visitors – my sister Rona's kids. They stayed for dinner. The excitement, and perhaps the food, made Aman's blood sugar jump up to 331.

He became very upset and worried. This obviously became his

excuse for not checking his sugar. He says it makes him more worried and as a result, it goes up. His kids helped him go downstairs to rest. He seemed so weak and fragile yet again.

He takes pills for his blood sugar, but the doctor in Kabul won't give him insulin to help him when it goes that high. He tells him to come to the office, so he can give him the insulin shot there. Doctors usually don't prescribe insulin to patients, because they're afraid that they will overdose and make things worse.

I insisted again on going with him to the doctor, to talk about that issue. I told him that I could teach him and his kids the procedure and the dosage. He still didn't want me to go with him. I think he was embarrassed by me, the "outspoken" sister. As an Afghan man, he is very traditional.

When I went downstairs to check on him and give him his B12 injection, he was asleep. His wife was sitting by his side, rubbing his feet. I sat by his head and started massaging his head and neck. His forehead was clammy and cold. I suggested that we take him to the hospital. His wife only said, "He won't go." She said that he would be OK by the morning. I didn't know what to do. How do you deal with someone so hardheaded?

I just sat there, flooded with old memories of my mother and father, and I started crying. This is the same house that my mom lived in, and I kept seeing her face. The nurse in me wanted everything to be resolved in a proper and professional way, but these people are so patient and are used to their own system of doing things. Who was I to force my ways upon them?

His wife again assured me that he was OK, and sent me to the guest room, which they had prepared for me with a bed, a computer desk and bookshelves. I came back downstairs to check on him an hour later. They were both sleeping soundly. He was not as clammy and cool and he was breathing easily. I felt better and went back to bed.

I called Tim the next morning, and talked to him about Aman's condition. He offered his support and tried to help me calm down. Aman had already gone to work. His wife Raheesa said his blood sugar was lower this morning. Ever since his conditioned worsened, his wife and kids have been trying to convince him to resign from his job. They were hoping it would now actually happen.

~~~

As much as Kabul has progressed, women still do not go places alone. It is only safe to go places with a male family member. My nephew took me places, but at times he was too busy with his studies or household chores, so I was stuck at Aman's house a lot, while everyone else was either at work or at school. But the next day, my nieces Sabrina and Fareeda, my nephew Paiman and I went shopping. We wanted to pick out some beautiful fabric to make some proper outfits for me to wear in Afghanistan. Everything I had packed was either too short, sleeveless, or too tight.

Retailers usually price things three times too high, so you have to work your way down to a fair price. Sabrina and Paiman didn't want me to do the bargaining, because they said my American accent was going to give me away. They said, "If the merchants hear you, they will assume that you are rich and raise the prices." So they did the bargaining.

My sister-in-law and her daughters are all custom seamstresses. During the Taliban regime, they had their own tailoring business at home since they couldn't go to work or to school. My nieces gave me catalogs to pick from, and said, "Which ones do you like?" I pointed to a few outfits, and they started measuring me and cutting fabric.

Then, they had me try on the finished products. Not for the first time, being here made me feel like I was royalty.

Aman came home from work, and he looked better. He said that his boss wouldn't accept his resignation. His boss told him since they had a work-related trip to India in a couple weeks, he could seek treatment over there, and then he could decide.

Aman has worked in the Government's Financial and Budgeting Office for over thirty years, doing surveys, statistics and auditing. He is the senior manager, and the boss doesn't want to lose him. He has gone to many different provinces, even during wartime, to conduct inspections. His life has been in jeopardy during those trips to the country's war zones; it's no wonder that the poor guy developed type 2 diabetes at age forty-five.

Every day, I talked with his family about his diet – how to avoid carbs and sugars, and how to give him the right meals and snacks. I had to remove the white bread and sugar from his side of the table. I tried to get him to walk as much as he could, and I walked with him around the front yard. Everyone encouraged him to drink plenty of water and tea, and I finally got him to monitor his blood sugar regularly. He started to do better after he finished up his six B12 shots and took vitamins. All that I could do was to hope that once I was gone, he would continue his treatment plan.

Aman's wife Raheesa and his oldest daughter Amena and I stayed up till 1 am talking about religion, mostly Islam. My sister-in-law studied Islam in college, plus she and her daughter both studied law. Amena is a judge in the Supreme Court. Raheesa teaches at college and she is the principle of an elementary school.

I had been studying world religions, especially Islam, but had so many questions. Most people don't know the real meaning of their religion, and they just follow in their ancestors' footsteps. They follow traditions, and not a lot of people want to discuss anything; they think if they question something, it'll be sinful.

"Does Islam discriminate against other religions?" I asked.

"The Quran does not discriminate. It accepts all the other holy books, the Torah, Zaboor, the Bible – we believe in all of them. But since Muhammad was the last prophet, we believe in everything he brought from God."

"So, why do these people go around killing people from other religions because they're not Muslims?" I said.

"The Quran doesn't say to kill other people. The true meaning of the Quran believes in peace and harmony. You can't kill another human being."

~ Twenty-Eight ~

My Two Worlds

One of my favorite trips this time was to the Salang Mountain range, where the trees are green and clean, and berries are blooming. There is a waterfall here on the Salang River that is fast and furious. It rushes down to a small river heading to the rocky Salang Mountain range.

It reminds me of the James River in Richmond Virginia, only faster and much bigger. No one dares to get into the Salang River. They don't have any rafting boats or anything. There was a young guy posing for the camera, trying to stand on top of one of the big rocks in the water. His friends were holding onto him by tying their shirts around his waist. At least they were careful. It was very funny though.

There were twenty-two of us on this picnic: Aman with his family, my cousin with his nine daughters, two sons, and his mother-in-law. We had a big feast of lamb kabobs, liver kabobs, *bolanis* (flat breads stuffed with potatoes and leaks) fruit and vegetables. I was very careful of not eating a lot of the meat, just to be on the safe side, as I sometimes get sick. My cousin's family had some pure fat lamb kabobs. Just watching them eat this was making my arteries constrict, but they were enjoying it.

Aman was having fun. We were playing cards and sitting by the waterfall under the trees. It was so peaceful and beautiful. We took a lot of pictures and videotaped. My nieces and nephews were also having fun. This was a good getaway after spending the last 3 days at my sister Rona's house in Shewakee. There is not much to do there, except sit, eat and drink tea. Rona and her husband still live there with their eleven children. Some are married and some are still at home.

I managed to help my young niece with her two-month-old irritable baby. He was very fussy. She continuously fed him every time he fussed, so he was being overfed. Plus, he had an ear infection. I talked to my niece about spacing out the feeding to at least 1-2 hours at first, and then 2-3 hours between feedings. She still couldn't help feeding him every half hour at first, but then she finally waited a little longer. We worked together on burping him by rubbing his back. I also massaged his ears and back. His ears started draining and the little cutie stopped crying and slept more.

I talked to my uncle who lives in Shewakee about opening a clinic there, since those people desperately need a clinic. They don't have a medical facility nearby, and most don't have any means of transportation to get to a hospital in the city. Therefore, a lot of sick kids and pregnant mothers don't see a doctor in a timely manner. There is so much unnecessary mortality as a result. He agreed, and offered my mother's share of the family lot to build a clinic on. It all sounded really hopeful, and we are still discussing how to make this actually happen.

I packed my things and went to Zaybah's house to spend the rest of my trip. They were getting ready for my nephew Zia's engagement party that night. Zaybah had just finished serving lunch to some close family members. She then took off to get her hair and makeup done. She asked me if I wanted to go have my hair done. I told her that I was OK with the way my hair was, and, "Since I live in America, I don't tend to overdo my makeup and hair. I would rather be simple."

She told me, "Make sure you put a lot of makeup on, lighter than the color of your skin," since everyone wants to appear white. I tried my best to apply more eye and face makeup. When she came home, Zaybah looked beautiful with her hair in an updo, and lots of face and eye makeup with false eyelashes. She looked so adorable. She looked at my makeup and told me, "It's still not enough."

I said, "Well it is getting late, so let's just go to the party."

Her husband and son joined us there. Once we got to the beautiful engagement party room, some of the in-laws were already present. Zaybah was right. They looked exquisite in their formal gowns, hats and makeup. I felt kind of underdressed. More people started to arrive, with more fashionable outfits and hair. One would have never thought that this country had gone through thirty years of war.

The couple arrived from the beauty parlor dressed in Indian-style clothing. She wore a Sari, and he was wearing long, silk embroidered jacket with soft silky pants and Indian shoes. They both looked so adorable. They went upstairs to freshen up and get ready to come downstairs. They were then ushered into to the party room, where they sat on a couch covered with a glittery cashmere throw and matching pillows, arranged on a stage with flowers.

The music started, and all the young girls, including Sonia, his sister, went out onto the dance floor, dancing so beautifully. Then, Zia's mom, dad and brothers were dancing. I joined them and was having so much fun.

I hadn't been to an Afghan wedding or engagement party for about ten years, and this was extremely important to me, since it was my nephew's happy occasion. Zaybah appreciated me being there to welcome guests, and entertain and make sure everything went OK. I was videotaping as much as I could even though they had a professional photographer. I was honored to be part of it with my sister Zaybah, since we have been so close all our lives.

Our relatives slowly arrived, later than everyone else, as they are more shy and reserved. They usually don't feel comfortable in formal hotel events like this, even though the men and women were separated. They mostly have their parties at home. That is what they are used to. But lately, with the new generation coming up with new ideas of glamour and celebrations in formal hotels, about half of my relatives are joining these parties now. I personally consider this to be a big achievement. The fact that the older relatives can be drawn out makes me happy. Even though they like to sit in the back and watch from the corners of their eyes, it is fun to see them enjoying themselves somewhat.

Zaybah, her husband, and their kids worked hard and spent a lot of money for the party. This is another Afghan cultural tradition – you see, it is the groom's family that pays for everything. Therefore, if you have a bunch of boys, you have to plan early and budget your money.

The couple now came back downstairs, wearing different outfits. Zia was wearing a black suit and white shirt. His fiancée, Treena, was wearing a sky blue, long trailed dress with spaghetti straps. She looked very elegant.

They were ushered around again by close family members, away from the kids who were running around unsupervised in the lobby. There was a little boy in the photographer's way, and they were trying to catch him. He just kept screaming and running away. I caught him and was trying to find his mother, but she was nowhere to be found. I finally took him to the party across the hall. His older sisters came, took him from me and thanked me. He finally stopped crying, and we were both relieved.

Then the couple exchanged engagement rings, and cut the three-layered white wedding cake decorated with pink roses. They served dinner at 10 pm, which is the normal Afghan way (they want you to starve before they feed you). There was a variety of rice dishes, and kabobs, mantoo (like beef dumplings with white and red sauce over it), fruit and vegetables. According to Islamic law, they couldn't serve alcoholic beverages, so we drank Coke with dinner and hot tea afterwards. The party lasted until just after midnight.

After the party, we all packed into cars and followed the couple to a holy shrine, to follow a tradition of the bride's family. The shrine was called Shadoshamsheri-Wali, and located near an intersection, so it was guarded by army men with machine guns.

The guards knew about the tradition, so they allowed us to enter and pray at the shrine. All the cars stopped, and everyone prayed before we got back on the road. On the way back, everyone was trying to race with the couple, and I was very concerned. No one wears seat belts, and the children are let loose in the car. Sometimes kids sit on the driver's lap, which to me is ultimately scary. That is the usual driving routine there every day, and that is the reason I don't drive in Afghanistan. I actually pray every time I get into a car or a cab.

Then about twenty of our family members followed the couple to Treena's parents' house to congratulate them. After they served us tea and juice, we came back home with a very sad groom. He was not allowed to stay with his fiancée, since they were not married yet, which of course meant no sleeping together.

It was 3 am by the time we got home, and everyone was exhausted. We all slept in the following day. I was happy for Zia, who got to go to his fiancée's parents' house to just hang out with his love.

My niece Sonia is such hard working person. She was up before anyone else, cleaning up. People still kept coming to congratulate the family. Zaybah was about to go crazy with so much company. We spent the day watching my videotapes; the professional one would be ready in a couple days, but this was good for now.

I got a chance to talk to Tim that morning. We missed each other so much, and I couldn't wait to go back to see my darling son and husband. The end of my trip was nearing, and I got excited, as I was finally able to get on Facebook. I guess now I am truly American, because I can't live without it.

I only had a few days left. We decided to go to the shopping mall and eat out. The mall was packed with merchandise and fancy clothes in different styles, mostly Indian and Afghan, with long sleeves and long skirts and evening gowns. I was hoping to find a T-shirt or a hat for my kids and Tim with a logo of Afghanistan. Unfortunately, I couldn't find any. I already had my traditional clothes that my nieces had made me, so I didn't buy anything, but it was fun browsing.

Zaybah and I usually go shopping together. We took a cab, and she sat comfortably in the passenger seat, beside the driver. Zaybah usually opens up a conversation with the driver. I guess that makes the fear of being in a cab a little less. It made me relax.

I have heard some horror stories about cab drivers in Kabul. They have kidnapped women, taken their jewelry and money, and even killed them. The cab driver that we had was twenty-two years old. He was a skinny man with long, dark hair that covered the back of his neck. He was unshaven with a dark complexion. He immediately started talking about his two wives and four children.

We didn't think he was even married, never mind having two wives at the same time. He said, "Once my 6-year-old son turns fifteen, I will leave both of my wives in the care of my fifteen-year-old son and go far away and find another wife." He said he could hardly support his wife and kids, since he is the only breadwinner, and that his life was too much of a headache at this point. Zaybah, Rona and I were appalled by what he was saying. We tried to talk to him about his responsibilities to his family.

Here is this 22-year-old guy who can't support his current family, and he is already looking for a third wife. I just shook my head.

Zaybah said, "Divorce your wives if you don't want to be with them."

He said, "No, that is impossible in Afghan culture." He is right. Men can have as many wives as they want, but according to their culture, they don't divorce.

The day before, Rona met a young man while she was waiting for Zaybah and me at the market. This young man said he was in love with a girl and wanted to marry her. But her parents required him to pay them $30,000 plus a car and more. Her parents don't even care about their daughter's happiness, just how much money they can get for marrying her off. That is equal to fifteen years' salary for an average white-collar Afghan man. He said that his brother was trying to help him financially, but he doesn't have that much money. So, he has to give up on his dream girl, because she is not allowed to speak up for herself.

It seems as if everyone is becoming greedy money-grubbers. People are desperate for money, so they have to get it somehow. I really feel bad for these girls, because they have no opportunity to defend themselves.

~~~

Finally, when my nephew wasn't busy, he accompanied me on a visit to the orphanage again. The director of the orphanage met me, and took me to two orphanages, one for the younger girls (grades 1-9), and the second for girls in grades 9-12. They have two more schools for the boys. I was amazed, as they had expanded from one orphanage to four orphanages in only a year.

My first sponsored child didn't come back after she went home at age eighteen. The director said they contacted the relatives, but got no response. She thinks they probably wouldn't let her continue her education, or perhaps they married her off. It was very sad. She had been there for a few years and had been doing very well in school. My second sponsored child was there though. I was so happy to see her and gave her a small gift.

The director told me there was another girl who was fifteen years old that didn't have a sponsor. She asked me if I could sponsor her instead of the first sponsored child. She seemed very nice and friendly, so I told her I would be glad to. I also brought a bunch of candy for all the kids at both schools. They were so appreciative and polite.

The orphanages are very modern and organized. They provide the kids' room, board and education. Some kids come from very poor families who can't provide for them. They have no means for any of the basic necessities of life.

This place is like heaven for them. They have a lot of Afghan and non-Afghan sponsors from all over the world. They have a good team of people working there, including the director. Before I knew it, it was time to leave. It is always sad to leave them there – they are all so adorable.

Then it was time to leave Kabul. I was glad to be coming home, but that meant leaving my first home and family. That is always the hardest part. My sister Rona, Zaybah and I had been having fun for the last few days – all three sisters together again. We missed my oldest sister Pari though. She is in Canada now.

That morning, after working for a couple of hours, my brother Aman came to Zaybah's house. He left work early because he wasn't feeling well. He had a headache and felt weak. He thought his blood sugar was high, but he didn't bring his machine to check his sugar; so typical.

I called his son Paiman and asked him to bring his machine. Paiman had his hands full with power lines being down on the ground, and he was waiting for the electric company to work on it. He informed us that he would bring it as soon as he could. We had Aman rest for a while, and he felt better once he got up. We had lunch, and he ate lightly. They were all helping me pack my clothes and all the gifts they had for me.

Zaybah seemed a little quiet today. She told me that it felt like someone had pushed her down, because I was leaving. I tried to comfort her, and told her I would be back before she knew it, in a year or two. That made her sadder, saying, "a year or two!" She told me that she wished we lived closer to each other, since we have so much in common. We were like twins when we were growing up. We still confide in each other more than anyone else. Zaybah is planning to renovate her home before her son Zia is married, since he is going to live upstairs. That project should keep her busy for a while.

My flight was at 2 pm, so we left the house at noon. Aman, Rona, Zaybah, and her family accompanied me to the airport. I had to say goodbye to them again. They were crying. I got emotional too.

As I was sitting by the window on the Ariana airliner back to Dubai, I noticed that the clouds below us were so beautiful. They were white, fluffy, ones that looked like uneven cotton piled-high into mountains. Some of them were thin and long, like opaque sheets. Every once in a while, a touch of a rainbow appears. I took some pictures of the clouds, but I don't think the photos do justice to the beauty of the sky.

As I am looking at the globe in front of me on the screen, the plane seems to be on top of the world. At one point, it appears that we have passed the North Pole. Looking out the window, I see mountains of snow, and what look like frozen rivers between the snowy mountains. Maybe it's Alaska?

On the other side of the world, my better world in the USA, my husband and children await. I know Tim is counting every second, because he told me he was following my plane online.

I could see the perfect blue sky from afar. The clouds started to get darker as the sun was setting. As we landed, the sun went down slowly and completely.

~~~

My two worlds: the one I was born and raised in – the one I will always treasure, filled with memories of my parents, my brothers, my sisters and my relatives. I will never forget the good times we had. Life was so simple, and people got along better. Time has changed everything though, and the effects of war and destruction have caused people to become insecure and greedy.

Then there is my perfect world, the one that I sometimes forget while I'm away, but I always appreciate after I return from Afghanistan. This country of mine, the United States of America, which is so beautiful and clean. We are spoiled by the conveniences and life's little pleasures that we take for granted. Imagine, if you couldn't drive a car, especially if you are a woman? Or, if you had to cover yourself from head to toe? Imagine not having running water or plumbing in your home, or public bathrooms.

Once again, I was greeted by my cool husband at the San Francisco Airport with his shaggy, unshaven face. He keeps it that way when I am away, because he says that he has no reason to shave. He brought me home, where I feel safe and content, and my son greeted me with the biggest hug ever.

~~~

Tim and me at the Santa Cruz boardwalk.

Me with my sister Zaybah in 2010.

The Salang River

At the Mehan Orphanage in Kabul.

With kids at the orphanage in Kabul, 2007.

~ About the Author ~

Anisa Mahmoud Ulrich grew up in Kabul, Afghanistan in the 1960s. She completed her nursing school education and became a refugee shortly after the 1979 Soviet invasion of Afghanistan.

She has been a labor and delivery nurse for over twenty-five years, and is married with four children. She is active in her local Chamber of Commerce, is a licensed RN and massage therapist, and a business owner. She frequently returns to Kabul to see her beloved family, but cannot wait to return to her "perfect world" in the USA. She resides with her

©Photo by Ashley Nichole Ulrich

family in San Ramon, California. This is her first book. Anisa can be contacted at anisa.ulrich@gmail.com.

~~~

~ Acknowledgements ~

This book would have not been possible without the support and encouragement of my wonderful husband, Timothy Ulrich, and my children, Nichole, Marin, Jay, and Zohra Lily, who helped write the back cover copy.

Thank you to my brother Zaman Mahmoud and his wife Ria for their support and for critiquing my manuscript.

I want thank my dear sponsors, Mr. and Mrs. Letcher and their children, for making it possible for me to write this book. Thank you Tina, for reading my story and for your wonderful feedback.

Thanks also to my friend Dolores Lloyd for her support, and for proofreading and critiquing my manuscript.

Words cannot express my gratitude to my editor, Lisa Drittenbas, for her professional assistance, not just for polishing this manuscript, but also researching every aspect of the story, and showing such an interest in making it the best story possible. She also formatted the book, designed the cover art and assisted in the printing. She has become my agent and a true friend beyond words.

And finally, this book would not be in your hands without the dedicated and friendly support of the Sacramento Public Library's I Street Press staff (istreet@saclibrary.org), volunteers, and their amazing Espresso Book Machine. Thank you!

~~~

Made in the USA
Charleston, SC
06 May 2012